THE SHEPHERD
AND THE
MORNING STAR

Willie Orr was born in 1940 in Northern Ireland. After a public school education, he had a variety of jobs, working for a time in the Belfast shipyards and also as an actor in theatres throughout Ireland. He then moved to Scotland and spent time in the Iona Community, before becoming a shepherd and later a teacher and a counsellor. A prolific writer of newspaper articles, poetry, plays and fiction, his previously published books are *Deer Forests, Landlords and Crofters* (1982) and *Discovering Argyll, Mull and Iona* (1990). He now lives near Oban in Argyll.

THE
SHEPHERD
AND THE
MORNING
STAR

TWO LIVES APART

WILLIE ORR

BIRLINN

First published in 2019 by Birlinn Ltd
West Newington House
10 Newington Road
Edinburgh
EH9 1QS

www.birlinn.co.uk

ISBN: 978 1 78027 588 8

British Library Cataloguing in Publication Data
A catalogue record for this book is available from the British Library

Typeset by Hewer Text UK Ltd, Edinburgh
Printed and bound in Great Britain by Clays Ltd, Elcograf S.p.A

Contents

Illustrations

To Justice for the Forgotten
Dublin and Monaghan

Two Conversations

I am cutting grass when he appears round the corner of the house. Two sparks of recognition flash in my head. First, it's my brother – instantly dismissed as I know he's in Canada. Secondly, my father – again dismissed as he is dead. Yet the resemblance is uncanny.

'Are you Willie?' he asks.

'Yes.'

'I'm your father's illegitimate son.'

'Good God!'

'No. Just James, I'm afraid.'

There is no doubt about it. He is more like my father than any of the family – the same impenetrable brown eyes, the same restless eyebrows, the same coal-black hair swept back elegantly over the ears.

I am seventy-three and he, I guess, is about sixty.

The phone rang one morning in August 1974.

'Hello. Is that Willie?'

A very well-spoken English lady.

'It is.'

'It's Julia. You may remember that we met earlier this year.'

Of course I remembered. My father had been visiting us in the West Highlands and had left rather quickly, claiming the need to attend a meeting. After he left, my wife and I decided to take the children for a day out in the car and, as we crossed the road to reach the car, another vehicle came towards us and stopped suddenly some distance away. I thought it was his car but, not sure, hurried the five feral children into the back of ours. His car started again and stopped behind us. Out of the passenger door emerged an extremely elegant young lady in a beige camel-hair suit.

'This is Mrs Stone,' he said, 'Julia Stone'.

'Could you not have come up a more convincing name?' I thought.

That must have been more than a year before the phone call.

'Yes, Julia. I remember.'

'Do you know where your father is?'

'No, I'm sorry. Have you tried the houseboat?'

'Yes. He's not there.'

'Perhaps he's in Ireland in the constituency.'

'No. Someone has tried there. Have you no idea?'

'No, Julia. We really don't keep in touch. Christmas, birthdays, that kind of thing. The last visit was the first for years. I really can't help.'

'You must have some idea. It's very important.'

There was an urgency, if not panic, in her voice.

'I'd like to help but there's nothing I can do.'

'He should be here. There are some very influential people here – John Gorst and other MPs. We're in Caxton Hall and we're about to get married but he hasn't turned up.'

'I see. I think it's just as well. I'm afraid he is still married to my mother.'

'What rubbish! What a dreadful thing to say. He's divorced.'

'No, Julia. You'd better check it out.'

The beginning of the end.

1

The bonfire spews flames and smoke into the night sky like the dragon's breath in my bedtime book. It roars and its heat burns my bare knees but I'm too excited to move back. Flames coil round the man in the middle of the fire, scorching his clothes and melting the peak of his hat. The flames light the faces of the people round the fire. Their eyes glisten and the teeth in their smiles glow like coals. They cheer as the man bursts into flames, his armband with the swastika falling from his arm. I look up at my grandmother who is clapping her hands and I wonder why she is crying and laughing at the same time. My mother is in the city having a baby and my father is still away at the war.

May 1945. The war was over. There were other bonfires all along the coast of Ulster. I could see them flickering on the sea. They were burning Hitler too. There would be no more sirens. That pleased me more than anything as I was afraid of that wail in the night and the drone of the German bombers, monstrous and malevolent in England. I had heard the distant whine of the bombs and I had seen houses burst open by the blast. I knew what could happen. When we heard the siren we used to scuttle downstairs, my mother carrying my sister, and I could see the fear in her eyes and in the white dimples at the corner of her mouth. It made me afraid to look at her. Sometimes, when the bombs were near, she grabbed my arm and hurried me along, her fingers trembling. Then I wanted to cry but I had been taught to be brave like a soldier, like my father.

'He will be home soon,' she used to say. I did not believe her because she said it so often and he seldom appeared.

Tonight I open my grandfather's diary, expecting to find a page welcoming the peace and mentioning my father's return to Ireland. The entry is brief.

'Mon 7th May – Slight showers. Working in garden. News this evening that the great European war has ended.'

A month later it records briefly that my father returned on leave and adds, 'Slight showers again.'

I'm tempted to say that I was confused by his return, that I was shy, that I was resentful of the intrusion or that I was pleased to see him, but the truth is that I recall only two emotions. He brought home a red metal toy crane with green winding string and a weighted hook. I was delighted with that. He said it came from Germany. In the evening I watched him from an upstairs window. He was down on the shore, kneeling on the ribbed sand, building little dams with his hands. He was completely alone in the dusk. I remember a feeling of sorrow as if I sensed his solitude, his need to turn away from us. Of course the memory could be tainted, for I have nursed it as a part of my portrait of him, the man who became leader of the Ulster Unionists, the Imperial Grand Master of the Orange Order, a public figure engulfed in media attention. His urge to find peace, to relish the tranquillity of a trout stream or the silence on the shores of Lough Gill, diminished as he ascended and, as that interest faded, I lost the only thing we shared.

I was nearly five on VE day and he has been dead for twenty years. I can't say that I knew him, for he spent most of his time away from us. I visited him in hospital when he was dying. I found an old man slumped in a chair, unable to raise his head or shuffle to the toilet. His brown eyes stared at the floor as if there was an abyss at his feet and he drifted in and out of disturbed sleep.

'We never talked much,' he said in one of his rare moments of lucidity.

'A great pity,' I replied.

It was, perhaps, his way of expressing regret.

I helped him to urinate into a cardboard bottle.

Twice he jerked out of sleep gasping with terror.

'They're coming!' he shouted.

'Who? Who is coming?'

The IRA? The police? The Orangemen? His women? Who knows?

I took his hand and stroked his head.

'They're coming.'

'It's the nurses, father. No-one else.'

The man who had spoken with such assurance and eloquence in the House was reduced to a pathetic creature haunted by shadows. For the first time I felt a strange affection for him. With all his faults – the philandering, the duplicity, the greed for power and acclaim – he had possessed irresistible charm and generosity and, far inside, that homunculus of romance and creativity which drew him into solitude.

How very different the patient from the man who returned from the war! I have a framed black and white photograph, a posed portrait, taken in 1940. It could be that of a film star like Omar Sharif. He is dangerously handsome, an affliction, in his case, which led to a succession of betrayals. Expertly lit, his sleek, dark hair merges with the black background and the light, filtered from above, emphasises his elegant jawline and sensitive lips. It is taken from the side and he is looking down as if absorbed in a book. A portrait of a thoughtful, creative young man – a poet or a painter or a musician but certainly not a reactionary politician.

I am intrigued, baffled even. How does a dreamer, a playwright, a young man entranced by the Celtic revival in Dublin before the war become a schemer, a ruthless manipulator, an equivocator? What changed the student who hired a horse-drawn caravan to explore the wilds of Galway with an actress who was not yet his wife? And what did the transformation do to her, for the actress became his bride and my mother? Was it a rapid change or was it a slow metamorphosis which she failed to notice till it was too late? So many unanswered, and perhaps unanswerable, questions.

There are, however, a few fragments which help to illuminate the dim territory of his past. There is a letter to my mother expressing his fury at De Valera's decision to keep Ireland neutral. Could this account for the change of allegiance? Or did his experience of battle and the blitz draw his sympathies away from the Ireland of Synge and Yeats to the Britain of Churchill and the King? He told us that he had faced the enemy in France. Yet his military record shows that he never left England. He was a wireless instructor in Windsor. No experience of battle nor in any more danger than the land girls in the fields or the families in the East End.

There is another explanation. He obtained a commission in the Life Guards and fraternised with eminent members of the

British elite. He had to borrow money from my mother to pay the prodigious mess bills of the cavalry regiment. Perhaps the lavish lifestyle and the affluent, influential company were so seductive that he could not relinquish them after the war. Certainly he developed a taste for extravagance which could not have been financed by the meagre and unreliable income of a writer. Any affection for Irish republicanism would have been anathema to his new companions. It is scarcely surprising that he worked for a position of power and influence on the conservative wing of politics. Yet I have no proof of his motivation. His ambition remains a mystery.

The war transformed us all. My memories, though few and no doubt coloured by time, are surprisingly vivid. Most of them are set in Camberley in Surrey close to where my father was stationed as a wireless instructor. My mother's brother, Desmond Hughes, must have been stationed nearby when he flew his Mosquito over the house and dipped his wings in salute. Desmond, the fourth top night fighting ace with more than eighteen victories, was awarded the DFC and, after the war, the AFC, and became Air Vice-Marshall. Desmond must have been the only air ace to have a stowaway in his aircraft. In 1942 his terrier 'Wee Scruffy' leapt into his Beaufort at the last minute and accompanied his master as he shot down a Junkers over the North Sea.

Another visitor to the house was Paddy Donnell. He used to carry me on his shoulders, acting as my steed, as we careered through the pine woods. The coarse epaulets of his Commando battledress scraped the back of my knees but I urged him ever faster, holding tight to his fair curls. Paddy became Lieutenant

Colonel in 47 Commando and led the attack on Westkapelle on Walchern Island to secure the landings in 1944. After the war he worked for the Shakespeare Memorial Company, organising tours in Eastern Europe. Mother's eyes always lit up when Paddy visited and she seemed to blossom in his company. She often spoke of him with great affection. He was my hero then and I still regret losing touch with him. Father was different. He had dark, angry eyes, a foul temper and was used by Mother as a threat and a means of control.

Out on the moor near the house there was an abandoned tank, its turret blackened and its tracks broken. What a temptation to a four-year-old boy! I walked out over the heather and climbed into the cockpit, pretending to drive against the Germans. When a young couple parked their car on the road and sprinted towards the tank I couldn't fathom why they were so agitated. I had not noticed the red flag on the hill and they explained breathlessly that I was sitting in a target and that shells could land at any time.

We didn't have many toys through the war but I had a superb source near at hand. There was a searchlight station beyond the woods with a Nissen hut where the men were billeted. They had to learn to recognise all the aircraft – British, German and American – and to help identification they were supplied with model planes. Many of these found their way to my collection so, by 1945, I could distinguish a Junkers from a Wellington or a Mosquito from a Messerschmitt. The men adopted me as a mascot, taking me to football matches and allowing me into the searchlight cabin at night to watch the beam and the small luminous screen.

Occasionally today the TV will replay films of the 'doodle-bugs' – the V1 and V2 – which were aimed at London but sometimes landed short of the target. I still react to the distinctive drone of their engines and recall the fear of adults when they were heard. Once, on recognising the sound, I crawled down under the blankets only to find, when the threat passed, that I was stuck, the bed being made too tight. That moment of panic returns at times when I remember the bombs.

Most people of my age respond to the wail of the sirens, always a signal for disruption as we hurried to hide under the stairs or in a shelter. Strangely, I never felt really afraid during the night raids but then our house had never been hit.

Towards the end of the war my mother taught me to change my sister's nappies so that I could show Father how to do it when we were returning to Ireland. I can't recall why she was remaining in England, unless she was pregnant at the time. Anyway Father, sister and I travelled by the night train towards Stranraer and I dutifully instructed Father on the art of changing a nappy. Halfway to Scotland we had to disembark and switch to a bus as the line ahead had been bombed. That was unpleasant in the cold dark night but worse was to come. When we reached Stranraer the Irish boat was delayed due to submarine activity and we had to spend the night on a covered pedestrian bridge over the railway.

My father's military career was quite uneventful. He joined the Royal Ulster Rifles in September 1939 and was sent for Officer Training. His first commission was with the East Lancashire Regiment and he was posted as a full Lieutenant to the Royal Army Corps in 1941. He was promoted to Captain to train cadets until he was posted as Wireless Officer with the Household Cavalry in April 1944. He joined the Life Guards in May of that year and, on his official release in June 1946, was granted the honorary title of Captain, a title that he used in his Parliamentary career. His records show that he was awarded the Defence Medal and the War Medal but no Military Cross. After the war he claimed to have been decorated with the MC and provided my mother with the MC ribbon which she kept in her jewel box. This fraudulent claim led to a serious rift in the family, as Desmond Hughes was furious when he heard, many of his closest friends having been killed on active service. Why my father claimed to have been decorated I could never discover and it will remain a mystery now that both he and my mother are dead.

After the war we lived in Donaghadee in County Down with my mother's parents. There I met a boy of my own age who was to become my best friend till he left Ireland to attend Bedford School in 1952. Jeremy (later Paddy) Ashdown had recently arrived from India, moving to a house just round the corner from ours. Discovering a neighbour with such an exotic, exciting background, I had to have him as a friend. He was a wiry, energetic, mischievous companion. We started primary school together and caused havoc in the classroom.

Sadly, my parents moved to a dismal hamlet called Blacker's Mill near Gilford, presumably because Father had become a Unionist organiser. The bleak Victorian house, surrounded by trees, was near a mill in which, I think, linen cloth was dyed, as the burn running past the house was frequently thick with colour. I had a small bike at the time and cycled to Moyallan school which was not far from the house. The heating in the school, consisting of iron pipes and heavy radiators, was far from efficient and many of us suffered from chilblains. Chilblains inside the leather boots which we wore were a form of torture. They were desperately itchy but you couldn't scratch them. I don't remember learning much there except how to hang upside-down from a branch by my legs. One of the brighter aspects of Moyallan was the journey home, as I could stop at Sally Best's house for fresh scones and jam. Sally was one of those splendid old country ladies who always kept treats in the cupboard for children.

It was in Blacker's Mill that my parents recruited a nurse to look after us. A fearsome lady who tried to impose strict discipline on both children and adults in the house. My sister and I resented this intrusion so much that we set off walking to Gilford to our grandmother's rectory, a considerable distance on the far side of the river Bann. I was six and she was four.

We marched past the school, across the white bridge, past the hatchery on Stramore Road, past Lauder's farm and even past the raucous geese that stretched their necks and threatened to devour stray children. Grandmother was wonderfully sympathetic when we told her about the nurse, gave us some barmbrack and milk, and sent us home by taxi to avoid PB's rage. We passed him as we returned, his car tearing towards the rectory.

We returned to Blacker's Mill and the harridan who had come between our mother and ourselves and whose intrusion convinced us that our mother had abandoned us to the cruelty of the nurse.

It was in that dismal hamlet that I first experienced the emotion of compassion. I was standing in a roadway bordered by high hawthorn hedges leading down to a crossroads. At the crossroads, about 200 yards away, there was an old man in a shabby raincoat and felt hat who was being tormented by three youths. They were pushing him one way and then the other and laughing at his distress. The incident passed quickly as a car approached but I remember the feeling of pity and I have often wondered about its origin. Was it spontaneous, a natural sensation arising from the realms of the subconscious or had it been absorbed from stories such as the Good Samaritan, a product of Christian ideology? Had I experienced something which, years later, helped me always to identify with the victim? On the other hand, perhaps the retrieved memory deceives me and I invent all the sensations to tell myself what I should have felt at the time. Anyway, the vision remains associated with Blacker's Mill.

2

'When you shall these unlucky deeds relate,
Speak of me as I am; nothing extenuate,
Nor set down aught in malice . . .'

Othello.

These words from the Moor's last speech will be a compass to steer me through the memories.

My father was known in his family as 'Poor Billy', shortened to PB, a soubriquet that I will use throughout this story. His father had him christened Lawrence Percy Story Orr but the entire village ignored the pretentious names and called him Billy. Born in Belfast in September 1918 just before the Great War ended, he was the first of four children. Not an easy birth. His father's diary shows the stress:

Poor Evelyn had a rather bad time of it. It was a difficult case and we had to call in Dr Hicks . . . I passed through an hour or so of great anxiety . . . there was a serious risk of it being dead born. As it is however they are both happily safe.

Giving birth at that time was always a risk and many mothers did not survive the ordeal. Evelyn was confined to bed for more than a week. PB's siblings said that he was not Evelyn's favourite son. Perhaps the difficult birth accounts for her indifference, and may explain his long fruitless struggle for approval in later years. He remained Poor Billy even when he was a prominent politician. On one occasion he was chasing James round the kitchen and she laid him out with a frying pan on the skull.

Evelyn Sarah Poe was said to be related to Edgar Allan, but I have never been able to confirm the claim. Her grandfather had married an Eliza Poe in Ballinasloe in 1852 but whether she was related to the American clan is not clear. Her mother, Kate, died when Evelyn was four, leaving her father to look after her and her two brothers. Kate is buried in Carnlough in a small, peaceful cemetery looking out over the sea to Scotland. She was only 26. When my sister took the name of Kate Story as her stage name, her superstitious aunt warned her against it but she persisted. She died aged 25.

Evelyn's father was a minister and lived till he was 96. A lean, irascible old man constantly at war with his housekeepers, there was nevertheless a twinkle in his eye and a mischievous grin beneath his silver Lloyd George moustache when he provoked an argument. Like many men of the cloth his temperament in the household was unknown to the parish where he was adored, particularly by the staff and patients of Belfast City Hospital as their honorary chaplain. Rev. Lawrence Parsons Story was a Galway man and a graduate of Trinity College, Dublin. He was Rector of Carnlough for twenty years after he married his second wife.

When Evelyn married my grandfather in Belfast in January 1917 he was described as a 'Clerk in Holy Orders'. He was 33 and had just made an extraordinary change in allegiance from Methodism to the Episcopal Church of Ireland. I have searched his diaries for an explanation but it remains a mystery. A glance at his father's long list of different parishes may provide a clue as, between 1869 and 1916, he moved 21 times between Ballyshannon in the south and Limavady in the north. Methodist 'itinerants' were moved regularly and perhaps my grandfather or his future wife preferred a more settled life. There is no record of his father's view on his disloyalty. The family had all been Methodists and both his uncles were ministers in that church. His father, James Orr, had been a radical non-conformist, becoming Vice-President of the Peace Society protesting against the Boer War. Evelyn, however, was Church of Ireland.

My grandfather's mother was from a hamlet near Roscrea in Tipperary. The founder of that dynasty was a farmer called 'White Willie' Drought of Ballybritt, known for his flamboyant attire of pristine white waistcoat and shirt. He poses for a photograph I have, standing nonchalantly with a leg crossed and one hand tucked in his pocket to expose his waistcoat, the picture of elegant wellbeing. Born just after the Napoleonic War in 1816, he lived till he was 81. My grandfather visited him shortly before his death in 1897 and found him in an immense four-poster bed, wearing a tasselled nightcap. I have his wife's diary, written in a small, spidery script to save paper, in which she records in June 1879:

This day my dear Margaret left me to be married to Rev. James Orr. I came home with a heavy heart and very disconsolate. Nothing would have induced me to part with her but that she was marrying a Godly man.

Margaret, her beloved daughter, gave birth to my grandfather in 1884.

The conversion of the Orr clan to Methodism was quite dramatic. One Sunday evening in 1843 in the township of Ballyreagh, County Fermanagh, a little girl, the daughter of Robert Orr, became 'suddenly and strangely affected' while singing hymns and passed out. She was put to bed and, on regaining consciousness, began to 'praise the Lord'. Robert was so affected by her response that he called people together for a prayer meeting. So many people attended that word of the event spread quickly till the 'whole country was roused'. All five Orr brothers were, as the Methodist history puts it, 'led to the Saviour' and two of them, including James, became itinerant ministers.

Both families were, of course, staunch Protestants. Evelyn's brother and her husband had signed Sir Edward Carson's Ulster Covenant in 1912 opposing Home Rule and refusing to recognise an All-Ireland Parliament, if it were imposed on Ulster. This protest movement led to the formation of the Ulster Volunteer Force (the UVF) and the shipment of arms for a revolutionary Protestant army. 35,000 rifles and 3,000,000 rounds of ammunition were landed in the ports of Bangor, Larne and Donaghadee and over 100,000 men were soon drilling openly across the province. The Tory party not only colluded in this armed resistance but supported it, a fact that is often forgotten in its condemnation of the armed struggle abroad. Rudyard Kipling donated £30,000 and published a belligerent poem in support of the Ulstermen, ending:

What answer from the North?
One law, one land, one throne.
If England drive us forth
We shall not fall alone.

PB, then, was brought up as a member of what was called the 'Protestant ascendancy'.

The family settled in Gilford, a small town centred on a linen mill which controlled the lives of the inhabitants. They rose in the morning to the wail of the mill horn and filed past under the watchful eye of the timekeeper at night. The mill owned the library, the cinema, the swimming pool and most of the dreary terraced houses. The mill bus collected the voters during elections and conveyed them to the polling stations. A town still lost in another century.

Rev. W.R.M. Orr started his ministry in Gilford in 1920 in turbulent times. The tragic partition of Ireland was imminent. There were sectarian riots in Belfast and killings were common throughout the province. Gilford was not exempt from the conflict. In September an Orangeman called William McDowell was murdered, an incident which immediately ignited sectarian strife in the mill. Convinced that Sinn Fein was responsible, the Protestant workers struck work and refused to return till the Catholics signed a declaration against Sinn Fein.

Two thousand Orangemen marched at the funeral at which my grandfather officiated and appealed for calm. 'To wreak vengeance indiscriminately on the R.C. population is iniquitous,' he wrote in his diary.

The trade union leader asked him to mediate so that the Catholics could return to work, an initiative which seems to have succeeded. Three men were eventually convicted of 'highway robbery' and murder and given life sentences. The jury having failed to reach agreement in a civil court, the case was transferred to a military court where they were found guilty.

There followed, however, one of the most sensational escapes in the history of Crumlin Road gaol. In May 1927 the three, with a superbly executed plan, overpowered warders and sped off into the night in a waiting car. One of them was caught soon afterwards but the others disappeared, apparently to run a garage in later years in the Republic. Material there surely for a movie.

I remember my grandfather from my childhood as a fearsome old man with a white beard and a Monaghan accent. He used to tell me stories from memory based on Poe's morbid tales or Conan Doyle's Sherlock Holmes. Sitting by the fire in his study at night with only the flicker of the flames to light the gloom, he would tell these tales with a conviction that added horror to the words. I can still recall shivering as he growled that sentence from the Baskervilles story, 'It was the baying of that hideous hound'. I think he relished the terror injected by his performances.

After these 'bed-time' stories I had to creep upstairs with a candle casting menacing shadows on the walls and leap into bed before the monster under the bed could catch me. There was a stair in the bedroom leading to a loft which was cluttered with paraphernalia from my father's childhood – a junior Orange drum emblazoned with 'Orr's True Blues', the skeleton of a parasol, a black ostrich feather stole, a massive cast-iron weather vane, a box of tin soldiers. I had climbed the stair on one occasion, pausing with every step to listen for wild beasts, and had glimpsed that cobwebbed scene from the top but, in spite of that exploration, the suspicion remained that there was something malevolent lurking up there.

PB had two brothers, James born in 1921 and Robin in 1924, and a sister, Katherine Margaret, always known as Lassie, born in 1922. While they attended state schools, he was sent to Campbell College, the Eton of Ulster, to be groomed for leadership, his fees apparently being paid by Evelyn's father. He became editor of the school magazine and secretary of the Dramatic Society, an elevation which may account for his infatuation with theatre when he enrolled in Trinity College, Dublin in 1937. At Trinity he was supposed to study Divinity but spent a great deal of time enjoying the company of thespians from the Gate Theatre. He was to be seen around Dublin wearing a green velvet jacket and yellow cravat, very much a bohemian of the Celtic Revival, writing romantic poetry and plays set in the west of Ireland after the fashion of J.M. Synge. A Tipperary newspaper described him as 'the distinguished author and playwright'. He became so entranced by the literary world that he left the Divinity Hall after a year, announcing that he was abandoning his course.

On hearing this shocking news, his father rushed to Dublin but was unable to find him. He tried the University, the hostel, the Savoy café and even travelled out to Sandford where PB had new rooms, but he was not to be found. The distraught old man had to return to Gilford without seeing his errant son. He did write a stern letter to him at his new address which had some effect, for he seems to have attended the occasional lecture, though they may not have been in divinity.

PB's main field of study was a young actress at the Gate Theatre called Jean Mary Hughes, a glamorous blonde, blue-eyed creature with what they called a 'full figure'. Jean had been brought up in a wealthy household which echoed with music. Her uncle was Herbert Hughes, a collector and arranger of Irish folk music and friend of James Joyce in Paris after his flight from Ireland on the publication of *Ulysses*. Herbert helped to produce the *Joyce Book* and Joyce wrote in response,

> The printer's pie was published
> And the pomes began to sing
> And wasn't Herbert Hughesius
> As happy as a king!

While in Dublin Herbert became involved in the new Abbey Theatre with W.B. Yeats and Lady Gregory, and Yeats was keen to employ him to write music for the theatre. However the appointment was opposed by one of the major patrons, Annie Horniman, because of Herbert's republican sympathies and her dislike of his music.

Herbert's first wife was Lillian Meacham, who was described as 'intellectually adventurous and sexually liberated' and 'the very model of a Fabian New Woman'. Her sister was Wendy Wood, later the renowned Scottish patriot, author and artist who, in 1932, led an assault on Stirling Castle, then an army barracks, tore down the Union Jack and replaced it with the

Lion Rampant. She shared an artists' studio in Edinburgh with her partner, Florence St Cadell. We have one of her small water-colours of a cottage on Iona, an island which came to mean much to all our family.

Herbert and Lillian's son was Spike Hughes, the jazz musician and music critic, who recorded as 'Spike Hughes and his Negro Orchestra', a title which would be frowned on today. His daughter, Helena, appeared in the first production of 'Look Back in Anger'. She and her sister used to stay with us in Camberley during the war, a great support to me when I was in trouble. GPs in those days had a sadistic habit of examining one's throat (even for a fractured ankle) by sliding the blunt end of a spoon down the throat and demanding an 'aahh' sound – an instant cure for malingering. If I was ill, I insisted that Helena, or her sister Angela, performed the task, as they were gentle creatures.

Jean's father, Freddy Hughes, was a superb pianist and accompanied John McCormack in early concerts. He was also a very wealthy industrialist, owning a large flour mill in Belfast. A small, volatile man, to be avoided on the golf course. He built a magnificent house called Whinstone on a promontory over-looking the sea near Donaghadee. One of the most beautiful interiors of the time, it was richly furnished with Tiffany glass, paintings by James Humbert Craig, Turkish rugs and dark oak furniture. Wide picture windows reflected the light from the sea, and the restful colours of the soft furnishings, chosen by Jean, matched every room – the blue room, the yellow bath-room, the green bathroom, the wide rainbow stairway. The music room with the concert grand piano was in Tudor style with dark beams and an immense stone fireplace with ingle-nooks. Scarlet velvet curtains. Everything designed to convey comfort and good taste.

What a contrast to PB's austere vicarage! Gloomy echoing corridors floored with brown linoleum. A black coal range in the kitchen. Thirteen pendulum clocks on the walls all chiming at different times. Black iron bedsteads with sunken mattresses and eiderdowns. Oil lamps instead of electricity and a water pump in the yard. The difference was striking, and no doubt lit a spark of aspiration in PB's mind.

Jean had studied music in London but had abandoned it in favour of the stage, joining Hilton Edwards and Micheal MacLiammoir in the Gate Theatre, Dublin. Sadly, I have no record of her performances, good or bad. PB, however, was entranced. They hired a horse-drawn caravan and travelled into Galway on a premature honeymoon, writing poetry and composing songs. Through one of the most inspiring parts of Ireland with its wild bog land and rugged coasts, thatched cottages and scent of turf, the memory of that journey remained with Jean all her life. It was all very romantic.

How she must have mourned the loss of that sensitive, crea-tive young man, enthralled by the West, when he was trans-formed into the politician.

While they were in Galway PB was given tragic news. His brother James, aged 18, had been drowned in a homemade canoe in Carlingford Lough. PB returned immediately.

The family had been on holiday in Killowen without their father, who had remained in Gilford to take the church services on the Sunday, and they had to endure the dreadful anxiety of the Saturday night of the tragedy without him. He was given the news as he left church and hurried down to Killowen to be with his wife. He wrote in his diary,

> We went to bed very miserable – with only some slight hope that James had been picked up by some passing vessel.

And on the following day,

> Sad day. We gradually came to the conclusion that poor James had been lost – very hard to realise . . . Evelyn in bed, badly overcome with the anxiety and the shock but wonderfully brave in spite of it.

My grandmother never really recovered from this loss as her son's body was never found. I have often tried to imagine the intensity of her grief and the anguish of those months wondering if her son might suddenly appear or be discovered. Listening for the postman or a knock at the door, waking in the night to hear a movement in his room, washing his shirts or finding his toothbrush in the bathroom, all the small reminders of his absence must have prolonged that dreadful suffering. Yet she had to cling to these, however painful, for to relinquish them would be confirmation of his death. I imagine her standing in his room, holding his blazer against her breast, folding it carefully, folding him away in her heart.

In the church in Gilford there is a plaque in the choir which reads,

In Loving Memory of James Herbert Thompson Orr who was lost at sea on the 12th of August 1939. "When thou passest through the waters I will be with thee". *Isaiah* 43.2.

This was the second great tragedy in her life, as her brother Percy was also drowned on active service in 1918. He was a surgeon probationer on HMS *Opal*, a destroyer which had taken part in the Battle of Jutland. In January 1918 she was returning to Scapa Flow in a blinding blizzard, when she and her sister ship the *Narborough* ran into treacherous rocks below the Clett of Crura off Orkney. She sank with the loss of all hands and there was only one survivor off the *Narborough*. The sea had claimed two of the men Evelyn loved, and it must have caused incalculable distress when her youngest son, Robin, having been rejected for the RAF, enlisted in the Royal Navy in 1941.

James was drowned in August. War was declared on 3 September and PB enlisted in the Royal Ulster Rifles on the 16th. He and Jean were married in October in Donaghadee and they sailed to Dunbar in Scotland, for his military training, eight days after the wedding. All this a whirlwind for Evelyn. I am left wondering how she coped. Her daughter Lassie joined the ATS, so she and her husband were left alone in the bleak Georgian vicarage in Gilford.

My grandmother was the person who influenced me most – grandparents often fulfil that role. She gave that unconditional love so essential to children. A small woman with a chignon, she exuded kindness and humour. I remember her smile and the quaint way she tilted her head to the side when she was teasing.

She sang at concerts and, when her husband's back was turned, smoked cigarettes, always declaring that she couldn't do without her ten 'Bachelors'. I often wondered if she saw me as a replacement for her lost son James. James is my third name and I was christened on the first anniversary of his death.

3

I was despatched to boarding school three years after the war when I was eight, a harrowing experience for a child. I'm sure that others who have suffered the trauma will recall that dreadful feeling of isolation and abandonment as the parents' car disappeared down the school driveway. I had only myself to blame. I had requested a transfer to Garth House School in Bangor, a boys' preparatory school, because my closest friend Jeremy Ashdown was there. There was, however, a more sinister reason.

The headmaster of the previous school in Belfast habitually inflicted an unusual and degrading punishment on his errant younger boys. Called into his study, they were ordered to take down their trousers and underpants and they were laid with bare bottom across his knee to be chastised with a ruler. For some reason there was always a female secretary in the room. I believe he was charged with offences some years later.

After a few incidents of this kind I stopped going to school, preferring instead to wander through the beech woods on the edge of the Lagan Canal. The calm silence of the woods broken only by birdsong and the chug of passing barges, the tall smooth tree trunks twisted like human limbs, the flickering sunlight through the beech leaves, all provided a sanctuary, a great green cathedral to shelter me from the adult world. The scent of beech haulm still reminds me of that escape.

There were horses on the towpaths then, hauling barges of coal or grain up the canal to Lisburn. The padding of the

Clydesdale's hooves and the clink of harness chains were the only sounds as they passed, the barges sliding silently through the water. In summer, swallows skimmed the surface for flies and the air was heavy with the scent of meadowsweet. The diesel barges were more exciting and, hitching a lift in return for handling the mooring ropes, I could stand in the bow and imagine myself as a sea captain. There were, of course, consequences of the truanting.

My parents had bought an imposing house near the canal at Drumbeg, south of Belfast. Drum House, a Victorian mansion, set in thirty acres of woodland with a massive monkey puzzle at the front door and an impressive columned portico. The staff consisted of a nurse, a kitchen maid, a housemaid, a gardener and a house boy who taught me to smoke Woodbines. The interior was tastefully furnished with red velvet curtains, Indian carpets and original oil paintings by Irish artists. Very grand and designed to impress influential guests and so to further my father's political career. My mother's father, Freddie Hughes, had agreed to hand over her inheritance in advance in order to secure the property. This was to cause bitter controversy after he died.

When they discovered that I had been missing school I was summoned into the inner sanctum of the vast sitting room. They were sitting on either side of the fireplace, waiting for an explanation. I stood to attention between them in my short flannels, determined not to cry. Father suddenly rose and towered over me, his eyes dark with fury, gimlets boring into my skull. He was a terrifying figure when angry. The inquisitor. He demanded an explanation. I didn't dare tell them about the headmaster. They would never have believed me. He was another adult after all, a respectable figure of authority. Besides, I was too ashamed to describe his punishment and was worried that they might approve of it. I thought it must be wrong but wasn't sure. I said nothing until Father gripped my shoulder and shook it. I started to cry and told him that I missed Jeremy so much that life was not worth living and that the only answer was to join him in his school. I was shocked when Mother agreed. He glared at her but capitulated. Perhaps rumours of the headmaster had reached them.

Drum House, in some respects, was a dismal place for a child, being so isolated, but its wooded grounds, hidden pathways and empty stables provided a private playground in which I could become a commando, an Apache, an Ashanti warrior or an air-ace. The distinction between reality and fantasy became blissfully blurred. My imaginary world was safer and more fascinating, at least until I changed schools and even then my imagination led to trouble.

Garth House in Bangor was a small 'preparatory' school with 50 to 60 boys, some of whom were day pupils. Those of us who boarded slept in dormitories with names which portrayed the ethos of the school – Churchill, Wavell, Montgomery, Mountbatten. I shared a dormitory with ten others, including Jeremy (later Paddy) Ashdown who had been a friend since 1945. As I had few friends in Drumbeg, Jeremy invited me to stay occasionally at his house in Comber. His father, Colonel Ashdown, had retired from the Indian Army to run a pig farm in County Down. The pigs were bred, reared, fattened on swill and slaughtered in a disused factory. I remember the mature pigs being stunned with electric shears behind the ears, their throats being slit, the trembling carcasses being gutted and then submersed in steaming baths to be shaved. The smell was revolting. The first visit to the slaughterhouse was enough. We preferred teasing the massive boars in the pens outside.

At Garth we were divided in two official houses – Danes and Vikings. However, beneath that, we organised our own tribes which often led to brutal and bloody battles after the fashion of *Lord of the Flies*. Dyaks and Ashanti, based in underground huts in the woods, would charge out to inflict maximum damage on the other tribe. One of the Ashanti, whose father had worked in Africa, brought in a genuine assegai, a weapon which, like a nuclear weapon, acted as a deterrent until it was confiscated by the staff.

The school building was an imposing, red brick Victorian villa set on a slope, with stone steps leading up to the pillared front door. The spacious grounds included a cricket pitch, a large vegetable garden and a plantation of tall trees which, although they were 'out of bounds', presented the young Tarzans with an irresistible challenge. The teaching block was converted stables some distance from the house where we ate and slept.

Many holidays then were spent with my grandmother in Gilford, she who loved me unconditionally. A time of fulfilment, of freedom, of waking without worry. Days of dreams, contentment, unanticipated pleasures. Mushrooms in the dew, fairy rings on the lawn, the scent of cypress trees in the sun, the dog's cold nose in the bed, blackberries in the hedgerows. Aware of happiness, unspoiled by wanting to be other than who I was. Another time, so far off, so inaccessible, an enchanted land unsullied by duplicity and desire.

I was in Gilford when my mother's father, Freddie Hughes, died in 1952. I travelled to the funeral in Donaghadee with my grandmother and Aunt Lassie. He was only 68 and had been admitted to hospital in Belfast for a minor operation. His wife, Hilda, was devastated and never recovered from the loss. It was my first close encounter with death, prompting a strange mixture of emotions. Being the only child there and surrounded by a smothering mass of grieving adults in black, I found the intensity of their emotions most alarming. At the same time, seeing the coffin and imagining him inside it, I was moved to tears of sorrow. Bach's 'Jesu Joy of Man's Desiring', which was played in the church, still reproduces that sadness.

The following January I was in school when we heard over the radio that the *Princess Victoria*, the ferry from Stranraer to Larne, had sunk off the Copeland Islands. I knew that PB had planned to travel that day and I was allowed out of school to stay with my grandmother in Donaghadee, where the survivors were landed, Whinstone being on a promontory by the sea. I was shaken by the ferocity of the storm, the wind being so severe that it was blowing the tops off the waves and forming what looked like a sea of glass. I imagined my father struggling to stay afloat in the freezing January water. It was such a relief when he phoned thoughtfully to say that he was still in London. Although he was safe, I went down to the pier and, when I saw the state of the survivors coming ashore, I was glad that he had missed the boat. I will never forget the skill and courage of the Donaghadee lifeboat crew. Only 44 0f the 177 aboard survived and two of PB's close friends, Maynard Sinclair and Sir Walter Smiles, perished.

PB and my mother occasionally took holidays in Donegal, driving across the border in a Humber Snipe with a caravan in tow. I usually persuaded Paddy Ashdown to accompany me as a diversion from the constant bickering of my parents. We would sit in the back seat, silently enacting the warfare in the front by making faces appropriate to the hostile dialogue between them. There were always adventures on these trips, often the result of PB's preference for inaccessible sites to park the caravan. He would drive miles down rough tracks, only to find that he couldn't turn at the end, an outcome that led to further snarling and hours of reversing. Once he parked on a beach and, as our arrival was after dusk, Paddy and I slept in the car. We woke in the night to find the incoming tide lapping round the doors. In a panic, we waded waist-deep to higher ground and waited in the dunes for the dawn. We didn't dare wake the parents.

Donegal was relatively unspoilt by tourism then. The barefoot children from one of the farms where we parked spoke no English, the only reply to a request for a can of milk being, 'What time it is, mister?' In spite of the strife in the car, there were moments of harmony. One evening we parked on the shores of Lough Gill, looking across to the Isle of Innisfree. The lake was almost calm, its dark surface rippled by a gentle breeze. Those lines of Yeats always return to me when I remember that dusk:

> There midnight's all a glimmer, and noon a purple glow,
> And evening full of the linnet's wings.
> I will arise and go now, for always night and day
> I hear lake water lapping with low sounds by the shore.

I have PB to thank for those memories and the love of Yeats. He took me to WB's grave in Drumcliff churchyard under Ben Bulben, and through the sands of Lisadell where Yeats used to walk with Countess Markievicz. In these surroundings he seemed to be a different person, a man longing for something he had lost, his nostalgia sometimes showing in a quiver in his voice and softening in his eyes.

At that stage I don't think I differentiated between my parents. I am not sure that I felt any particular affection for either of them. Placement in a boarding school effectively severed any deep emotional attachment and the introduction of nannies to look after the younger children deepened the chasm. Sharing feelings with parents, or indeed with any adult, was not an option. I lived largely in my own head.

Returning to boarding school after the holidays was always torture. Garth House's declared purpose was to prepare 'boys, between the ages of 7 and 14, for the English and Irish Public Schools, and for the Royal Navy', essentially for the Common Entrance Exam. Like many other prep schools, the emphasis was on the building of 'character' through discipline and wholesome sporting activities. There was no place for gentler emotions like sorrow. Pupils learnt to 'play the game' and to recognise what was 'not cricket'. Even day boys were expected to comply with school rules at home by being in bed by 8 o'clock if under 12, and 8.30 if older. A note had to be provided if this rule was broken.

In the early years we were taught by a tyrannical old lady who did her utmost to terrify her pupils into learning anodyne poems like 'Up the Airy Mountain' by William Allingham and 'The

Owl and the Pussy Cat'. Miss Swanson was the sister of the school's founder and ruled by the cane. Her unique attire betrayed a stubborn resistance to elegance or fashion – shapeless hand-knitted woollen dresses in drab colours, flat shoes and fawn stockings. With her short, cropped silver hair tied back with a black Alice band and her hooked nose and chin, she would not have been out of place on the blasted heath in the Scottish play. We knew her as Nelly. Universally disliked, she set out to make the lives of the small boys as miserable as possible.

I remember having to sit beside her at a long dining table with Paddy Ashdown immediately opposite me. I had just taken a drink of milk when he pulled a face to make me laugh. I couldn't laugh with my mouth full of milk and I couldn't swallow. With a sense of impending doom I fought to control the urge to laugh but, alas, it overwhelmed me and the mouthful of milk exploded all over the table. Nelly's reaction was immediate, stabbing my hand with her fork. This was followed by a hundred lines, 'I must not eat like a savage.'

The Headmaster, Captain Hutton, came to the school during the war from the British Army in North Africa. Untrained as a teacher, he did nevertheless inspire us with an interest in literature and history. Those of us who boarded will remember the evenings round the coke stove where we made toast and listened to 'Hutty' reading the Hornblower books and other 'suitable' novels. Having been a boxer for Trinity College and a cricketer at senior level, he also promoted sport as a vital part of the curriculum. During one boxing session in my later years he ducked into one of my punches and knocked himself out. The spectators stood aghast, thinking I had killed him. Cricket under his command was strictly a gentleman's game. I was once suspended from the team for daring to celebrate at the crease on scoring a century. The kisses and embraces seen on pitches today would be anathema to his generation.

Thanks to him some of us developed a passion for swimming, one of our contemporaries, Peter Pedlow, later competing for Ireland. A remarkable family, the Pedlows: Cecil playing rugby for Ireland and the Lions, Peter swimming for the country, Ken playing golf at that level and Desmond a rugby player for Ulster. We learnt to swim in Pickie Pool, an outdoor saltwater affair which could be so cold that we emerged with feet and fingers white. Character-building. It had one advantage, though. When we invited other teams to compete against us, they were paralysed by the cold. We had a swimming team of eight which Hutty used to squeeze into his Morris Minor to compete with other schools.

4

During my time in Garth my parents moved from Drum House to a house called Ossory in Newcastle, presumably to be in the heart of the constituency. Ossory was not so grand as Drum but was still an impressive Victorian villa with a large garden. It was there that my sister first experienced the thrills of performing. During the summer, travelling entertainment companies used to stage shows on the bandstand by the seafront. Known as the 'pierrots', they were an extraordinarily versatile group. Their programmes contained melodramatic sketches, comic pieces of music, dancing and singing. To attract audiences they also included a local talent competition, which Mary couldn't resist as she was bent on becoming a famous ballerina at that time. My reactions to her appearances tended to swing from admiration for her courage to embarrassment as she pirouetted unsteadily across the stage. She did win a prize occasionally, but never for her dancing.

Newcastle in summer was a wonderful place for a youngster. We could hire rides in ex-army landing craft – DUKW's or 'ducks' – and speed down over the sand into the sea. There was a travelling circus which set up its tents in the local park or the 'demesne' as we knew it. There was one of the longest beaches in the county just north of the Slieve Donard Hotel and an outdoor swimming pool. We had freedom in those days to wander where we liked without causing our parents any concern. I went fishing with a rod made of an old tank aerial, I climbed Slieve Donard,

I was a spitfire pilot flying in the sand dunes, a commando in the woods, a boxer in the garage – having no punch-bag I used my young brother. Rinty Monaghan, the world champion flyweight from Belfast, was my hero then – I listened on the wireless to his fights and his routine singing of 'When Irish Eyes Are Smiling' after the bout.

My parents, always keen to impress, used to have dinner parties for local dignitaries. On one occasion their guests included a bishop. Unfortunately my father's wayward brother – my uncle Robin – was home on leave from the Navy and, having spent the afternoon in local hostelries, joined the company. He was indeed dangerously intoxicated. When the soup was served my mother watched aghast as sleep overcame him and his head, sporting a profuse black beard, sank slowly but inexorably into the soup. That same evening he was found in the driving seat of an empty bus at the bus station and, when asked what he thought he was doing by an irate inspector, replied that he was going to Gilford.

'This bus isn't going to Gilford,' the Inspector warned him.

'It is if I can get the f——n' thing started,' he replied.

He was escorted off the premises.

He was my favourite uncle, always getting into scrapes, always an embarrassment to my upwardly mobile ambitious parents. He had served on HMS *Rodney* during the war and had been on the convoys to Archangel. He had an intense aversion to young first officers, referring to them as 'snotties', and had a tendency to adjust their facial features if they annoyed him. He spent most of his Naval career gaining good-conduct stripes, only to lose them a few weeks later after assaulting a 'snotty'. He was a member of the boxing team but I think he preferred the battles ashore outside the ring.

During our last few days in the school Hutty called the senior boys to his study to educate us in the physiology of sex. When we were told that 'the man inserts his John Thomas between the woman's legs' we had to bite our lips to suppress the laughter.

We knew about sex – with boys that is. Intimacy with girls remained a mystery. Older boys initiated us to the pleasures of 'self-abuse' as it was called, and we relied on photos in *Men Only* and *Lilliput* as sources of fantasy. Some still believed that semen was actually brain fluid and that masturbation led to madness. Homosexuality was still illegal of course, but many prep-school boys had illicit love affairs.

We did have other forms of entertainment in the dormitory. We had a competition to see who could tell a story which would keep the others interested over as many nights as possible. The prize, of course, was the admiration of one's peers. The penalty for talking after lights out was a thrashing. I lost count of the number of times I was caught. I tended to get so carried away in my stories that I failed to notice the glow of the matron's cigarette in the doorway, only to be shocked into silence by the command, 'Report to the Headmaster in the morning, Orr'. I was a slow learner.

Jeremy Ashdown left to enrol in Bedford, later joining the Marines and the Special Boat Squadron. When I finished in Garth my parents informed me that I would be attending Campbell College in Belfast as a boarder to be shaped for leadership. By that time, however, I was living with my mother and grandmother in Donaghadee and had discovered girls. One of them, when I was on the point of passing out during a long embrace, suggested that I should breathe through my nose when kissing, a technique which I have found quite useful ever since. Puberty is a stormy time for any youth, but to be incarcerated in a boys' boarding school, having just tasted the fruits of Eve, was a barbarous form of cruelty.

I fell in love during the holidays and, for the first time, experienced at first hand the gulf between the two tribes of Ulster. At dances we learnt to detect members of the opposite community by signals as insignificant as a name or school. Bridget or Kathleen might indicate a Catholic. Billy a Protestant. A school with 'Saint' in its name, a Catholic. We used to develop a kind of intuitive ability to categorise, an invisible antenna, an instinct that led to early detection of the other tribe. That radar was a mechanism which we absorbed unconsciously from infancy. It penetrated our system like a malignant organism, spreading irresistibly, insidiously, till we were completely contaminated. Spread from our elders in little toxic references, hints, nuances, glances, expressions of contempt, it swarmed in our blood, claiming us for our race. Those who suddenly realised what was happening and, horrified by the infection, tried to expel it, still carried its traces into their future, their minds pock-marked by the experience.

My first love went by the name of Mitzi, which was not helpful. She was a 'blind date', whom I met in the back row of the Tonic cinema in Bangor. I was boasting how I used to steal my lunches from Woolworths when she confessed that her father was the manager. In spite of that shaky start we went out together for a year or so. Much to my father's consternation, she was a

Catholic, a fact which troubled neither of us till the priest inter-
vened and put an end to the affair. I was, of course, heartbroken
– the first cut is the deepest as they say – but also resentful of her
church's interference.

That first love was not the blazing furnaces of later affairs but
a calm sea in which we sailed together without a need for direction, a moment of our lives – all too brief – when we drifted
through the days savouring the times together. When every
meeting was like a new beginning, when every holding of hands
was another bond, when her every feature was a discovery. She
was as precious to me as the break of each day, a work of art not
to be defiled, a sculpture fashioned by the gods. To lust for her
body would have been sacrilege. When we walked through the
woods at night the limb-like beeches seemed to bend in rever-
ence and enclose us in an impenetrable cocoon. After we parted
I often returned to the places where we had stood and held each
other, mourning the loss.

I detested Campbell College. The uniform reflected the
austerity of its ethos – a white shirt with detached studded collar
starched to sever your neck, black tie, flannel trousers (snail-trail
ones on Sunday) and black jacket. Junior boys had to have all
three buttons done up, middle school two and only seniors were
permitted to have open jackets. Juniors suffered humiliation,
oppression, brutality and abuse from the prefects. The only
females in the building were the maids who had to endure
several hundred lecherous glances in the corridors. A member of
the rugby team (call him Sinton) used to visit one of the more
generous young ladies in her quarters. Making his way to her
room one evening he was shocked to meet an elderly (and we

thought decrepit) teacher emerging from the maid's room next to hers. Equally startled, the old man shuffled past muttering, 'Evening, Sinton'.

Nothing more was said.

A couple of the teachers made the place bearable. Davey Young, the English teacher, who had been a fighter pilot, introduced me to Thomas Hardy and seemed to sympathise with the more 'challenging' students; and Mr Mitchell, a History teacher, who devised an escape route from the school for me. Most of them, however, belonged to another century and were determined to stamp out any signs of non-conformity. Some of us, asserting our distinct (and probably detestable) identities, rebelled. We altered our flannels to resemble drainpipe trousers, attached black velvet to our collars, cut the black ties to look like string ties and wore Tony Curtis haircuts with Ducks Arses at the back. Toff Teddy Boys.

I teamed up with another revolutionary to plan an escape to Australia. We arranged with the skipper of a small coal boat in Belfast docks to work our passage to Scotland by shovelling coal from the hold. From there we intended to hitch-hike to London and buy a £10 ticket to Sydney. Sadly, my comrade had leaked the information to his sister who passed it to the parents, and we were arrested on the dockside by the harbour police.

I became a day boy in my final year and travelled with this companion by bus to Belfast, both carrying in our bags our 'civvie' clothes. On the journey we decided whether to attend school or travel on into the city, the latter normally being the more attractive option. When in Belfast we wandered the streets, watching for beer delivery lorries from which to win a liquid lunch. He would walk up the outside of the lorry holding his bag open and I would follow, lifting the bottles into the bag.

Outside school I met Spam, a delinquent teenager whose proficiency in the art of petty theft I had to admire. Together we launched a minor crime wave in Donaghadee but were never caught stealing cigarettes and alcohol. From him I learnt some astonishing details of sexual behaviour. His success with women and his complete lack of respect for them were notorious. Being untutored in psychology, I could never understand why women, knowing how they would be treated, were attracted to him but they seemed to be hypnotised by his outrageous promiscuity. Still, Spam was my hero. From him I learnt about street fighting, a form of combat quite unrelated to the gentle art of boxing under Queensbury rules taught at school. He had a habit of starting fights outside dance halls and then calling on me to help. I carry a scar to remind me of those affrays.

Infected by Spam's contempt for convention, I committed a cardinal sin. We were living with my grandmother Hughes at the time who purchased her gin by the crate. Discovering that bottles of Gordon's Dry London Gin could be opened easily and the tops invisibly replaced, I developed a cunning plan. I removed the tops, emptied a quantity of gin from each bottle into an empty one of my own, substituted water and replaced the tops, convinced that my grandmother would never notice. I had underestimated her ability to sniff out contamination of her favourite tipple. She never forgave the offence and treated me with a degree of diffidence for the rest of her days.

I lasted only two years at Campbell before being asked to leave. On my last day the Headmaster called me into his study and, studying the somewhat repulsive specimen over his glasses, started the short meeting with the comment, 'We don't like each other very much, do we, Orr?'

I did not bother to reply.

Father was furious when I left, warning that I would receive nothing more from him – not that he had millions to dispose of anyway, but rather a large amount of debt.

5

PB, as I've said, returned from the war a different person, sloughing off the attachment to romantic Irish culture and nostalgia. He joined the Ulster Unionist Party, initially taking a position as organiser in Iveagh and, in June 1949, becoming a candidate for South Down, a constituency which included his parents' home town of Gilford. In the competition for the candidacy he made much of his military career and his rank of Captain. Jean, of course, had to take on the role of an Ulster politician's wife, dedicating Orange banners, opening bazaars, attending meetings. In the election of 1950 his agent was Brian Faulkner who was later to become Prime Minister of Northern Ireland. PB declared his opposition to nationalisation – 'ruinous to our national economy' – state control, Communism and, of course, any hint of cooperation with the Free State. During the campaign I made my first political speech from a platform, urging voters 'to come out early and vote for Orr' – memorable rhetoric indeed!

PB won the 1950 election with a majority of 16,000 over Jack McGougan of Irish Labour. There was a victory parade the night after the count. A lorry decorated with bunting, Union flags and the victorious politician with his team drove triumphantly through the town, the cold night sky lit by flaming torches and vibrant with the wails of an Orange pipe band. A night to remember. The night that he launched a political career which was to end suddenly and ignominiously.

His maiden speech in the Commons was on the subject of the fishing industry on which, of course, many of the villages such as Kilkeel and Annalong along the coast of South Down depended. The debate had been opened by Bob Boothby, then MP for East Aberdeen, claiming that the fishing industry was in 'a very great crisis', suffering from rising costs and Norwegian imports. PB urged the Government to establish a White Fish Marketing Board to control the influx of foreign fish and support the ailing industry, a suggestion which could be mistaken for socialist intervention. His speech was welcomed by J.J. Robertson, the Socialist member for Berwick and East Lothian, and the proposal was taken up by the Government. For his efforts he was elected as Honorary Secretary of the Conservative Party Fisheries Committee.

Later that year he made his position clear on the unification of Ireland, a stance to which he adhered throughout his time in Westminster. Addressing the Primrose League in Caxton Hall he declared, 'The idea that Ireland was one nation was fallacious because it was not one nation, had never been and was never likely to be. The only nation to which the whole people of Ireland ever belonged was the British nation.'

An inflammatory statement in many Irish communities.

He stood again in October 1951 against a nationalist candidate, Gerald Annesley, a Protestant landowner who believed in a united Ireland. He managed to reduce PB's majority to just short of 11,000. There were few republican MPs then. Cahir Healy, who had been interned in a prison ship on Belfast Lough in 1922 for his views and again in 1941, was elected in Fermanagh and South Tyrone, and Michael O'Neill in Mid-Ulster. Even in

Derry the Unionist was returned unopposed. These results, however, concealed the increasing militancy of the republican movement. In 1954 it carried out a raid on Gough Barracks in Armagh, carrying off a haul of guns and ammunition, and in the following election two Sinn Fein MPs were elected, both of whom had been imprisoned for the attack. PB and other Unionists in Westminster had an urgent meeting with the Home Secretary in which they declared that they were shocked by the outbreak of terrorism, '. . . but, in view of the camping, drillings and assemblies that have been going on recently in Eire, we are not surprised.'

We were living in Tufton Street near Westminster Abbey at that time in a flat just below Christopher Soames and his wife Mary, Winston Churchill's daughter. Having two very young children in common, my mother and she instantly became friends. PB invited Christopher and his wife over to Ulster for the Twelfth demonstration and took Christopher to see the mock battle at Scarva, a colourful affair in which the Battle of the Boyne is re-enacted complete with exploding muskets and a 'King Billy' on a white horse. I'm not convinced that Christopher was impressed.

I hated London, preferring to spend holidays with my grandmother in Ireland. Those were the days of the 'smog', an alarming experience when the sulphurous fog was so thick that you could not see the kerb on the pavement and traffic came to a standstill. You always imagined that some carnivorous monster would suddenly loom out of the fog to spring at your throat. I was caught out a couple of times and sneaked into a news theatre till the poisonous cloud lifted. The flat was just across from Big Ben and I could never get used to the monotonous clangs which seemed to reverberate through my bed. We were supplied with a division bell to summon PB across to the House in the event of a three-line whip, and this would shatter my dreams regularly. I do not recall Tufton Street with any affection.

I remember PB being most concerned about a demonstration organised by Gerald Annesley on his estate in Castlewellan. Annesley had invited a Judge Mathew Troy, an Irish American and vehement republican, to visit Ireland. Troy drove through Castlewellan town in an open car behind a parade of IRA veterans with tricolours flying. Twenty bands and 20,000 people attended the meeting in Annesley demesne, a turnout large enough to alarm any Orangeman.

One of PB's most memorable adventures occurred in 1955 after he had been elected for the third time. An Orange march was organised along the Longstone Road near Annalong, a quiet fishing village under the Mourne Mountains. With the Ballyvea bandsmen marching in their brilliant new uniforms and the banner of the lodge swinging over them, the Orangemen set out to march to Annalong. They were halted halfway by a barrier of boulders and a crowd of republican protesters. The bandsmen stopped and, for a moment, there was silence. The 'noble Captain Orr' assured the marchers that they had the right of way and they stepped forward under a hail of stones. Six hundred armed police, naturally protecting the Orangemen, charged with batons drawn. The Chief Inspector, hit on the head, fell but others, some streaming with blood, carried on. The ballad continues:

In the midst of all the riot,
Twas glorious to see
The bandsmen walking steadily on
Lead [sic] by their gallant MP.
And when they reached the village
The cheers near reached the sky
And to the platform Captain Orr
Was carried shoulder high.

What a hero! The ill-prepared protesters were driven off, of course.

His private life by then forced him to begin weaving a web of deceit which eventually entangled him in catastrophe. My mother had moved back to Ireland, so he could pursue a secret life in London. He formed a relationship with a young lady who rescued him from his financial chaos and helped to organise his affairs. I will call her Marion after Robin Hood's lady. This illicit liaison was to last for twenty years, providing him with stability and a comfortable and caring home. An honest, open and sensible woman, she did not deserve the treatment with which he was to end their life together.

To create the impression that PB was nothing but a rogue, a dissembler, a ruthless philanderer, would be a distortion. Like Hamlet holding the skull of Yorick I have his character in my hands and I'm conscious of the other side of his nature. He was a man of irresistible charm and good humour. He had a fine tenor voice, could accompany himself on the piano and sang sentimental Irish songs with moving conviction. He painted too, like his hero Churchill, but the pictures were sadly lifeless, as if the artist feared to reveal himself, the small chrysalis of the real person hidden far inside a public shell. He was most himself when trout-fishing on the streams of Antrim or the hill lochs of Donegal. I hope his ladies saw this side of him.

In Ireland his wife, traumatised by his rejection, turned to religion and became involved in faith-healing. Having visited Iona and charmed the leader, she founded her own community near Bushmills. Here she enticed the sons and daughters of wealthy Ulster families to seek refuge from the cruel world. They were often fragile, fractured, lost young people in need of care and therapy. In the community they received the laying on of hands from the leader, who had now assumed the role of confessor, priest and healer. Their parents, relieved to find a placement for them, paid for their keep, a contribution which allowed Jean to maintain the lifestyle to which she was accustomed. There is enough evidence to suggest that the entire project may have been fraudulent. Certainly it smacked of sorcery and exploitation.

History will record little of note in PB's political career through the 1950s. A researcher would have to trawl through many pages of Hansard to find his name linked with anything significant. He was elected secretary of the Ulster Unionist Council in Westminster in 1953, but had to offer his resignation three years later owing to 'pressure of work'. He was Grand Master of the Parliamentary Orange Lodge and Grand Master of England and had embarked on an ambitious project of writing a history of the Orange Order.

Linked to his wartime experience in wireless, he became a parliamentary advisor to Pye Radio and Chairman of the Mobile

Radio Users Association. In 1954 he was rather unjustly accused of favouring his broadcasting commitments over the plight of the unemployed in his constituency, receiving a rebuke from Jim Callaghan for the alleged failure. The complaint came from the Newry and District Trade Union Council whose spokesman claimed that PB had failed to attend its Conference on Unemployment. Clearly jealous of the attention broadcasting was receiving, the spokesman complained that PB had made 'more than a hundred interventions, speeches and questions' in the House on broadcasting and commercial television, yet had neglected the unemployed in South Down. The accusation was unjust as PB had given a reason for missing the Conference, but I know that anything resembling Socialism was anathema to him.

In 1961 he travelled to Moscow for the Soviet Trade Fair, motoring through Europe with John Stanley of Pye and John Gorst, whose wife, Tatania Kolotinsky, was Russian. They were delighted to find that the cameras used by Soviet TV were Pye models. The visit had been encouraged by Harold Macmillan who was trying to improve relations between Britain and the Soviet Union during the Cold War, and Reggie Maudling, as President of the Board of Trade, took PB and seven other MPs to Moscow. Pye Radio had a stand and a van in Red Square. PB's links with the company were organic, as he had been given a personal loan to cover his debts. The 'Pye loan' was occasionally mentioned in hushed tones in the family.

PB seems to have enjoyed the 'jolly', meeting influential people like Sir George Harvey Watt, Aide-de-Camp to the

Queen, and Comrade Lublin of the Supreme Soviet, and having dinner with Eric Bessborough, a director of ATV. Although he was quick to notice the 'drabness of shops, the slowness of lifts and the general inefficiency of service' and 'a woman barber with a cut-throat razor', he found Moscow to be a 'wonderfully beautiful city at night'. He had time to visit the Kremlin and the Bolshoi Ballet, but the place which impressed him most was the Monastery complex of Saint Sergius in Zagorsk. It is a remarkable settlement with its array of blue 'onion' domes and golden spires, but his notes on the visit hint at an appreciation of more than the architecture. Certainly there is reference to the icons, the frescoes and the wonderful choir in the cathedral, but he composed an extraordinarily romantic poem, reminiscent of Yeats, for a lady who accompanied him there.

ZAGORSK 1950s

When you are very old, my love,
And when serenity has stilled
The changing magic of your face
Will you remember then
The dappled sunlight in Zagorsk
The painted gateway
And rooks around Byzantine domes?
Will you remember then
The pigeon's wings before the church
The rapt and mystic faces of the worshippers within
And will you hear again the ageless music of the choir?
Or will it all be then

So very long ago
And all that heart-breaking beauty
Be buried like myself beneath the busy years?
Or could you just remember
And believe that someone loved you
And loved you more than all the rich enchantment
Of sunlight in Zagorsk
And loved you more than life itself
When you were young
So very long ago.

Apart from Pye, he also provided political assistance to British Lion Films Ltd through a difficult time. Roy Boulting wrote to thank him in May 1964, saying that he had 'done so much for us as individuals, for British Lion as a company, and the independence of film-makers generally.'

Sir Michael Balcon, the Chairman, also wrote to express his gratitude. At that time the company was largely owned by the Government's National Film Finance Corporation, and Ted Heath was keen to see it privatised. Clearly, as was seen in the debate on 16 January, PB had been in discussion with Ted Heath to advance the case for the Boulting brothers group, which included Baroness Wooton and David Kingsley. His efforts helped it to secure the bid. Roy Boulting gave him a pair of inscribed gold cufflinks for his help.

He did oppose Britain's membership of the EEC, along with other Unionists, believing that economic integration would lead to political union and eventually to a United Ireland. The phrase 'Treaty of Rome' was enough to send any Orangeman into a lather. However, he did not mention this in the debate on the second application for membership in May 1967, but instead concentrated on Britain's loss of sovereignty. Membership, he argued, would lead to 'an unacceptable loss of sovereignty. What is different about this loss of sovereignty from other losses is that this is an irrevocable loss. It is a loss of sovereignty which can never be regained.'

His preference was development of links with the European Free Trade Area and the Commonwealth. All very familiar arguments in view of the Brexit referendum. He was, he said, going to join his 'pair', Michael Foot, in the 'No' lobby. 'It will be an extraordinary thing for me to find myself in the same Lobby as the Honourable member for Ebbw Vale but there I shall be.'

In this he was following Enoch Powell, who had led the debate with the same arguments.

The fears of the Unionists in Ulster at that time are still as prevalent today, and have led to a bisection of the province from north-west to south-east in the 2017 general election. PB's South Down constituency has elected a Sinn Fein MP with a 2,500 majority, a transformation which, as the saying goes, would make him and Enoch Powell, his successor in South Down, turn in their graves.

In the 1950s and early 1960s the IRA was largely invisible, apart from the attack on Gough barracks. The raid on Felsted School in 1953 was perhaps more typical, when the IRA broke into the cadet corps armoury and stole 98 rifles, 10 Sten guns, 8 Bren guns and various mortars and magazines. The old van used to escape was so overloaded that it was noticed and the haul was recovered by the police. The IRA's main weakness was that it had little support from the public. At the end of the following decade, however, the spotlight swings again in PB's direction, as Northern Ireland erupts into bloody sectarian violence.

6

In May 1966 a petrol bomb was launched through the window of a house next to a Catholic off-licence in the Shankill Road, Belfast. Matilda Gould, a 77-year-old widow, died in the inferno. Her house had been daubed with slogans such as 'Popehead', 'Remember 1690', 'This house is owned by a Taig'. Tragically, Matilda was a Protestant. The police identified the perpetrators as members of the UVF, the Ulster Volunteer Force which, a month later, declared war on the IRA, warning that 'known IRA men will be executed mercilessly'. And so it began. In June four young Catholics were shot in a bar by the UVF. None of them had IRA connections.

The UVF had been revived after Prime Minister Terence O'Neill had dared to invite Sean Lemass to Belfast, a gesture seen by the loyalists as a step towards Armageddon. Like Grendel out of the Fens the figure of Ian Paisley rose out of the shadows to form the Ulster Constitution Defence Committee, an umbrella organisation for all kinds of sinister and unpleasant activists. On the opposite side the Civil Rights Association was formed in 1967 to campaign for 'one man, one vote' to correct the injustices of the blatantly unfair Ulster electoral system, to abolish the partisan 'B Special' police force and to end discrimination – the kind of discrimination I had earlier found in the shipyards. Much of its approach was based on the non-violent policies of the American civil rights movement, but it provoked outrage in the loyalist tribe which saw it as a republican front. A tragic misconception.

In October 1968 the Civil Rights leaders held a march in Derry. The brutal attack on the marchers by the police was filmed by Irish TV and the pictures of men, women and children being beaten to the ground flashed round the world. Gerry Fitt, a Westminster MP, was shown with blood flowing from a head wound. It is said that this image changed Martin McGuinness from a typical youth to a committed activist. The rage and hatred in the faces of the police horrified most civilised viewers. That night the Bogside in Derry exploded as rioters stoned police cars, threw petrol bombs and broke windows, a scene that was to become all too familiar on TV. In Westminster Captain Orr praised the police as 'the finest police force in the world' and tried to maintain the convention that Northern Ireland affairs should be left to its Parliament at Stormont.

Worse was to follow. Another Civil Rights march organised by university students set off on New Year's Day 1969 from Belfast heading for Derry. It was attacked several times by gangs of loyalists wielding iron bars, cudgels studded with nails, bottles and planks. The young women at the rear were singled out for special treatment, some of them being driven into the nearby river at Burntollet Bridge. The collusion of the police in these attacks was again shown to the world. This was the real beginning of the 'Protestant Backlash'. The situation was clearly out of control.

Terence O'Neill set up a Commission to investigate the causes of the unrest and Brian Faulkner, by then a Stormont MP, resigned and other Unionists demanded O'Neill's resignation. O'Neill, who had tried to calm the Civil Rights movement with reforms so limited that they merely provoked its members and infuriated the Loyalists, dissolved Parliament. In the subsequent election O'Neill was returned, but the Unionists were deeply divided – some hoping for reform, others regarding it as the path to unification with Eire. To emphasise their disaffection with the latter, the pipeline carrying the main water supply to Belfast was blown up and the main electricity sub-station at Castlereagh was also destroyed. The UVF was proving that the IRA was not the only group capable of guerrilla warfare. O'Neill resigned in despair. In the Commons debate which followed on 22 April 1969, when Bernadette Devlin made her rousing maiden speech, Captain Orr had nothing to say.

Later that year, however, as the violence on both sides escalated, there was another major debate in Westminster and he spoke passionately in defence of the Union, the police and even the B Specials, pointing out that the Ulster Protestants regarded the latter as 'one of the greatest guarantees of their liberty' – many civil rights campaigners saw them as thugs.

PB also opposed direct rule by Westminster, describing it as 'unworkable' and 'no better recipe for civil war' – an inflammatory statement in the circumstances. He was attempting to defend the indefensible. The Ulster government, being notoriously partisan, had failed to deal with discrimination and disorder, the police were seen by the Catholic community as a blatantly Unionist force and the B Specials were out of control. So dire was the situation that the Dublin government decided to send army field hospitals to the Ulster border to deal with Catholic casualties.

It was estimated that 650 Catholic families were burned out of their homes in one night and such attacks were not confined to Catholic homes. In the summer of 1969 more than 1500 Catholic families and 315 Protestant households were forced to leave. The British Army was sent in, initially welcomed by the Catholic community, but it was the beginning of a long and tragic involvement as the troops were gradually forced into a battle with the Provisional IRA.

Sunday 30 January 1972 will be remembered with shame by the British Parachute Regiment, leaving a bloody stain on its history. A march in Derry against internment without trial was brought to an end by the regiment opening fire on and killing 13 unarmed protesters. TV viewers all over the world will not forget the picture of a priest waving a handkerchief as a white flag as he tried to take one of the wounded to safety. 'Bloody Sunday' was made into a film with James Nesbitt and eventually, after years of denial and cover-up, prompted an apology from the British Prime Minister. In the debate on the catastrophe PB's only contribution was to ask if the control of the RUC was to be transferred to Westminster. Perhaps he was not called by the Speaker or perhaps, as an ex-serviceman, he could not bring himself to criticise the Red Berets nor to believe that they could act in such a barbaric manner. I have no idea how he felt about the slaughter, a subject assiduously avoided in our conversations.

In the course of the debate the fiery republican MP Bernadette Devlin was so incensed by Reggie Maudling's defence of the troops that she crossed the floor, slapped him in the face and pulled his hair, justifying her action later by declaring, 'I did not shoot him in the back which is what they did to our people.'

Ted Heath, who had little time for PB and the Ulster Unionists, suspended the Ulster Parliament, announcing that all matters of security were to be transferred from Stormont to Westminster. Naturally this infuriated the loyalists, but also created a climate of fear in the nationalist community which suspected that it would become the target of loyalist rage. In fact the inter-tribal violence did continue to escalate, becoming ever more vicious and inhuman. Most people will remember the appalling scenes on TV of severed limbs, torn flesh and bloodied pavements, but what was not shown was much more horrifying. One man was kidnapped, tortured, castrated and left to die with his genitals in his mouth.

It was at this point that Enoch Powell appeared in PB's constituency. I know that my father admired Powell – his oratory, his intellect and his knowledge of the classics – an admiration which I didn't duplicate. Powell's interest in the province stemmed from his opposition to the EEC membership which the Ulster Unionists also opposed vigorously in the House of Commons. He developed a lasting friendship with PB and Jim Molyneux from about 1970.

The first meeting he addressed in South Down was in January 1971 in Banbridge, not far from my grandfather's parish in Gilford. Powell used the meeting to reiterate his opposition to the EEC and to accuse the British government of deceiving the electorate. He maintained that, while the manifesto declared an intention to explore membership, the real plan was to join. He warned that membership would lead to higher food prices in order to sustain the 'large peasant populations' of the three largest European countries. It was essentially a message for the Conservative Party in Westminster, although it did contain a passing reference to the misrepresentation of the Unionist community,

You are the victims of misrepresentation . . . hardly a day passes that physical force is not used against you, the people of Ulster. But far more dangerous than any physical weapon, more deadly than the machine gun and the bomb and the petrol bomb, is misrepresentation. What the enemies of Ulster rely upon for their success is to make you misunderstood by your fellow subjects in the rest of the United Kingdom.

I'm not sure that the victims of the atrocities would have agreed with him, but he received loud applause from the 1,000 who attended the meeting.

In June the following year he arranged to attend a mass Orange and Unionist parade and rally with PB near Banbridge, but my father was taken ill and his place was taken by Lord Brookeborough. Powell apologised for PB's absence and, according to the local paper,

There is only one thing which diminishes my happiness at being here and that is the fact that my friend and comrade in the House of Commons, Captain Orr, cannot be here because of his recent illness . . . he has asked me to bring you his greetings and affection and I have the greatest happiness in doing this.

In July, incensed by Willie Whitelaw's meeting with the IRA, PB, as leader of the Ulster Unionists, wrote to the *Times* expressing:

grave alarm at the failure of the Government to prevent widespread murder and anarchy in a part of our country ... a variety of private armies has been deployed in the streets ... since March 24th 156 people have lost their lives ... by negotiating with the IRA the Secretary of State has nor only broken faith with the majority in Ulster but given an accredited status to men who employ murder for political purposes ...

He demanded an end to the 'No Go' areas and that the Army should be given a clear mandate to support the civil power in law enforcement. The letter was also signed by Enoch Powell and other Unionists.

Finally an attempt was made to lay the foundations of a new structure in the morass of Irish politics. The White Paper of March 1973 brought together not only the warring sides in the north and the British state but also the Irish government. The Paper was enacted a few months later. Power-sharing was imposed on Northern Ireland and, after elections in June, an Assembly met in July. After inevitable wrangling over positions, an Executive was formed. The most contentious proposal was that of a Council of Ireland which, in spite of its limited powers, was seen by the loyalists as a step towards a United Ireland. An inter-party conference was held at Sunningdale in England to discuss the Council. And, in a debate in the House of Commons on 10 December, PB denounced the Council as a deceit.

Its effect is to deceive someone. If the purpose of the agreement [at Sunningdale] is better law enforcement and fruitful economic co-operation in Northern Ireland, the erection of this vast edifice tends to deceive the people of the Irish Republic that a united Ireland is round the corner. If, on the other hand, there is another motive, it is the people of Ulster who will be deceived.

Surely an executive based upon such a flimsy type of deception is bound to be unstable and is bound to feed violence on both sides?

Ted Heath chastised him, strongly repudiating all PB had said and insisting that there was no element of deception and no 'vast edifice', the Council's Executive having only 14 members.

Three days later PB continued to oppose the Council, claiming that any attempt to enact any constitution regarding the Council in the House of Commons would essentially require the agreement of a 'foreign power' (Eire) and that that foreign power had made no promise to amend its constitution (which did not recognise Ulster). The Council was an 'embryo parliament' of a united Ireland – 'the beginning of the end of the Union and the beginning of a united Ireland', 'a sentence of death with a stay of execution'.

Having enjoyed the cultural freedom of Dublin as a student and embraced the music and drama of the Celtic revival, he now rejected every connection with the Republic in an attempt to retain the votes of his South Down loyalists. This commitment, however, did not prevent his betraying them in his personal life. 1974 was to be a disastrous year for him and his ladies.

The year started badly for those hoping for reform in Ulster. The Unionist Council voted to reject Sunningdale and Brian

Faulkner resigned as leader. The first meeting of the Assembly after Sunningdale broke up in chaos. Kennedy Lindsay leapt on to the table used by the clerks, grabbed a microphone and harangued the opposite benches. Ian Paisley and his team seated themselves on the government front bench and had to be removed by police. Any hope of an agreed solution to Ulster's misery was fading. To add to the uncertainty, Ted Heath called a General Election.

PB retained his seat but with a vastly reduced majority of 3,500 over his nearest rival Sean Hollywood of the SDLP. Interestingly, Hugh Golding of the Republican Clubs polled only 3,000 compared to PB's 31,000. A sinister figure, however, loomed on the horizon. Enoch Powell attended a conference of Paisley's United Ulster Unionist Council, a group vehemently opposed to Sunningdale. The first General Election of 1974 brought in a new government in Westminster with Harold Wilson's Labour party failing to gain an overall majority. The eleven Ulster Unionists, known as the 'Ulster 1st Eleven', were not popular on the Labour benches, particularly with Merlyn Rees, the new Northern Ireland secretary.

In March the loyalist Ulster Workers' Council warned Rees to pay heed to the results of the election in Northern Ireland, hinting at widespread civil disobedience and grave industrial consequences if the new government proceeded with Sunningdale. Enoch Powell joined in the fray, describing the power-sharing executive as 'a dummy, a wreck, a water-logged hulk', rhetoric designed to impress the Unionist elite in PB's constituency of South Down, a seat which he was to take over on PB's sudden departure. The dispute between the British

Government and the extreme loyalists was rapidly becoming dangerously insoluble. In May the UWC called a general strike demanding fresh elections and an end to Sunningdale.

Harland and Wolff's shipyard came to a standstill, the Sirocco engineering works closed, 400 workers in the aircraft factory joined the strike. Yet the response was not impressive. The UWC had to resort to intimidation and set up road-blocks to persuade strike-breakers to conform. Within a couple of days the shut-down was almost universal and the UWC threatened a complete power blackout. The 'loyalists' were taking on the state to which they claimed loyalty.

In the House, Captain Orr described the strike as:

> . . . the most serious situation that has arisen in the whole of the history of the past four years. Most people in Ulster dislike a political strike and intimidation and they understand that the Government should not concede to that kind of pressure. Yet should it not concede to the ballot box? The people of Northern Ireland want a chance to express their views.

Careful not express his own views, he supported the aims of the strikers. The situation, he said, was 'but one step short of civil war' and was 'out of political control'. The strike brought down the Ulster Executive and obliterated any hopes of a peaceful solution to the violence and bloodshed.

In the midst of all this occurred the greatest atrocity in the history of the Troubles. On 17 May 1974 two UVF units left the north and travelled to Dublin in hijacked cars. At 5.30 pm, just as city workers and office staff were heading home, two massive explosions ripped through the streets, killing 26 innocent civilians, including 20 women and two baby girls. Half an hour later another car bomb exploded in Monaghan, killing a further 7 civilians. The terrorists responsible have never been brought to justice and there is very strong evidence to suggest that the British security forces in Ulster colluded in the crimes. A group rightly called 'Justice for the Forgotten' still campaigns for the truth. There is no recorded comment on this outrage by the MP for South Down.

The UWC strike was called off after the Executive collapsed and administration of the province was transferred to Westminster. Through that summer PB continued to campaign for a pledge from the Labour Government that Northern Ireland would remain part of the Union.

> There will not be peace, nor a return to order, nor will the Army commitment be reduced, until there is stability. It must be stability based upon the clear will of the majority with magnanimity to the minority.

Exactly how that 'magnanimity' was to be enshrined in law was the insoluble problem of the time.

As summer faded into autumn so the end of PB's career drew nearer.

7

I started work in Harland and Woolf shipyard in Belfast as an apprentice electrician in 1956. That was the beginning of my real education. There were 27,000 workers in the yard then. Now only the giant crane stands as a memorial to the skilled men who built the *Eagle* and the *Canberra*. The yard was built on an island, causing pandemonium at starting time and in the evening as the masses of cloth-capped men hurried south for the city. The workforce was very clearly divided. Catholics could not get apprenticeships – neither in the yard nor in any of the major engineering firms – so the skilled men were all Protestant with a fervent commitment to maintaining their privileged position, and the helpers were Catholic. You were careful not to board the wrong bus and, if you did, to keep quiet. What was strange, though, was the bond between the owners of industry and the skilled workers, the cement that bound them being the Orange Order.

I can't say that I enjoyed the transition from private school to the harsh reality of the world of work. An Oxo tin of cheese and onion sandwiches instead of a three-course lunch; an awakening at six and a six-day week. Still, I could smoke and swear and drink and wear what I liked and was paid £3 weekly. A different world of mountainous hulls, towering scaffolding, echoing alleyways, chains, hawsers, acetylene flames, flashes, metal dust and steam. I swaggered around in jeans obtained from an American sailor, welly boots turned down at the top, a sky-blue denim shirt with American cigarettes in the pocket and a suitably belligerent expression like James Dean.

When a ship was first launched the bare steel hull, stripped of any fittings or insulation, acted like a giant refrigerator, so the first task in the morning was to light a fire to keep warm and brew up. The prospect of trying to bend heavy electric cables round bulkheads with freezing hands kept us by the fire till the gaffers appeared. The gaffers wore bowler hats which, we were told, were reinforced with steel in case subversives dropped missiles on them. Watch for the bowlers on the Orange parades.

When the caulkers started buffing with grinders the din was deafening. We could barely hear each other and the noise still rang in our ears when we went home at night. It was a relief when I was moved to refit a Canadian aircraft carrier called *Bonaventure*. It was almost warm on board and the stately silence was disturbed only by the gentle hum of generators and the genteel intercourse of the happy workmen! We were on the ship during its tilting trials when it was tested by heaving it with hawsers from the quay to its superstructure till it listed like a stricken vessel. This created a bizarre sensation for the men in board, who had to walk at an angle along the corridors. If you forgot to lean, you fell and had to endure the guffaws of the other men.

As apprentices we were supposed to attend night classes two evenings a week, a demand that interfered with my social life so seriously that I was forced to give up the habit. One thing kept me in the yard for a while – a girl in the tracing office whom I could see at lunchtime. We met at a St Valentine's dance. I was surprised when she agreed to go outside the hall, thinking that she was too attractive to be seen with me. A face from the Renaissance with brilliant blue eyes, elegant brow and fine jawline, a figure slender and shapely but not voluptuous. Not too perfect, though, with a sharp, pointed nose and small, pinched mouth reminiscent of a shrew. Outside, against the wall, she kissed with polite restraint as if she longed to be passionate but didn't dare to release the dangerous emotion. Yet she did not object when I slid my hand down her thigh and slowly, with infinite care, rolled up the back of her skirt till I touched her skin. I remember how the fabric slipped sensuously over the nylon stockings. Two years we stayed together. My first girlfriend. We were living in Bangor at that time in a red-brick house above Ballyholme Yacht Club. PB's visits became less and less frequent and my mother took to her bed in protest with all kinds of imaginary illnesses, leaving my sister and me to run the house. Mary meticulously kept a record of the supplies purchased for the house, noting the price of each item and adding up the total weekly. The sums, however, bore no resemblance to reality and we plunged into debt. My mother employed a young lady to look after us. Unfortunately, she was most attractive, so Mary and I laid on a candlelit dinner for her with a generous amount of wine and mood music. After the meal Mary went to bed and I was left to seduce the young lady. She left the next morning.

This was the time of Bill Haley and the *Blackboard Jungle*, of listening to Top Twenty on Radio Luxembourg 208 metres, of EPs and jive. I bought my first record player and practised rock beat with drumsticks on a cane chair. When *Rock around the Clock* came to the cinema we rocked in the aisles and rioted when the manager stopped the film. There was a sense of freedom, of casting off the stuffy ethics of the older generation, of well-deserved self-indulgence. Splendid times. Not that we were unusually affluent. I had my £3 a week and gave half of it into the house for keep.

In November 1956 our urbane Prime Minister, Anthony Eden, decided to invade Egypt in response to President Nasser's nationalisation of the Suez Canal. Naturally the price of petrol soared and the Government announced a plan to ration fuel. My delinquent friend seized the opportunity, persuaded me to join in his enterprise and we launched our nefarious business under cover of darkness. There was a dance-hall nearby so we siphoned parked cars while the drivers were in the dance and sold the fuel, a most lucrative business. It did, however, leave a nasty taste in the mouth.

It was obvious to my sister and me that the marriage of our parents was failing. PB placed an advertisement in the local paper indicating that he was not responsible for his wife's debts. This was scarcely surprising, as Mother frequently sent me to the back door to placate irate tradesmen demanding payment. 'Tell him I'm not well and to come back next week.' Our parents' problems were not discussed with us and PB's visits were always made as pleasant as possible by pretending that everything was fine. There came a point, however, when they met in what was the Midland Hotel in Belfast in an attempt to reach agreement on finance. It was a bizarre experience for me, as I was taken along as a witness and finance was never discussed. They sat in the lounge gazing out of different windows and talking about trivia. Their last son, Christopher, had been born in 1953, the product of the death-throes of the marriage.

Keen to prove that I was a man vibrant with machismo, I left the shipyard and joined the army. The recruiting officer in Belfast, having asked about my education and learning that I could almost speak French, immediately assigned me to the Intelligence Corps. Private Orr 23514091 appeared in Maresfield Camp in Sussex where I learnt very little about military intelligence but a great deal about scouring pots in the camp kitchen. I have three vivid memories of my military career.

There was a recruit from Manchester, unfortunately called Kelly, who could not master the art of marching. In spite of the usual patient coaching by the platoon corporal, his leading arm always swung in time to his leading leg, a practice which led to chaos in the ranks. At the passing-out parade he was placed in the middle of the squad with the rest of us drilled to ignore his movements. I remember the sweat on his pimpled face, the mist on his milk-bottle specs and the grim set of his jaw as he fought to step in time. I think he was transferred to MI6.

Those were the dying days of national service, so the Intelligence Corps attracted a haphazard collection of recruits, some completely oblivious of their military setting. We had a lieutenant whose main interest was the staging of scurrilous plays in the camp. He rewarded our help with his projects by sneaking us out of the camp in the back of his Deux Chevaux covered in blankets to enjoy riotous nights in Brighton. We had no interest in learning to kill people or in torturing them without leaving a mark. Today we would be classed as 'enemies of the people' and marked for elimination by MI5.

The third memory is a visit to my father in London. Given a 48-hour pass, I arrived at his fourth-floor flat in the early evening hoping for an invitation to stay for the night. I knocked on the door. Hushed voices but no reply. I knocked again and announced who I was. This time the letterbox opened and my father's tremulous voice issued from the aperture.

'Is that you, Willie?'

'Yes. I was hoping for a bed for the night.'

The letterbox shut. A whispered conversation inside. It opened again.

'Well, Marion is here and she is afraid of men.'

Marion was his PA.

'But she knows me.'

The letterbox shut and opened again after a minute or so.

This time an orange ten-shilling note appeared.

'Go and find somewhere to stay and I'll see you in the morning.'

I departed, disappointed that he could not trust me with his secret. I liked Marion and did not mind him living with her. We all knew that his marriage was comatose, if not already moribund. I spent the night in a West Indian club in Soho listening to Little Richard and smoking weed, a very rare substance outside the City at that time.

Joining the army was a mistake. Having manipulated an exit from public school, it was foolish to imagine that I would enjoy the discipline of the armed forces. I was far too spoiled. As teenagers my sister and I had enjoyed complete freedom, our mischievous self-indulgence having no limits. Children whose parents separate often feel that, because they have been hurt, they deserve some reward, rebellious hedonism being the most attractive form of this. We did revel in the freedom – its consequences for us both came later. In the meantime I managed to convince army psychiatrists that I was unsuited to a military career and was allowed to leave.

My mother and the other children had moved to a dismal house in Tennyson Avenue on the other side of Bangor. It had three storeys, the top storey of two rooms being my domain, a private eyrie to be visited only with consent. There I could entertain young ladies and cover the ceiling with bizarre paintings. I had a massive Crucifixion hovering over my bed. My sister and I occasionally threw parties, inviting selected thespians like Jimmy Ellis, Betty Hogg and Colin Blakely. On one occasion I had invited an attractive young actress from Belfast with the intention of inviting her to my eyrie for seduction. In the middle of the party I noticed that she had disappeared and that another actor, who was living with us, was missing at the same time. Suspicious of the coincidence, I climbed up to the eyrie and found them in my bed. Outraged, I summoned him out of the room and felled him with one blow. PB, who had been visiting, heard the thud and, emerging from the single bedroom below, called out, 'What's happening up there?'

'I hit Desmond,' I replied.

'Oh, I see,' and scuttled back to his burrow. The actress never accepted another invitation.

On another winter's evening the thespians in the party decided that a midnight swim would be fun, so, in a dangerously inebriated state, we made our way down to Pickie Pool which was, of course, closed. Nevertheless, we climbed in and plunged into the ice-cold water in our clothes, hurriedly leapt out, gasping for breath, and sped back to the house. Arriving drenched but delighted in the porch, we were barked at by an infuriated Betty Hogg, accusing us of endangering the life of her husband, Jimmy Ellis, who was just recovering from a chest complaint. Clearly he was none the worse.

My sister and I had become involved in Bangor Drama Club which was one of the most successful clubs in the North, producing at least half a dozen actors who became professional – Colin Blakely, who later became a star with the National, Denys Hawthorne and Doreen Hepburn among them. I remember shows like *My Three Angels* and *Teahouse of the August Moon* in which my sister played the female lead as a geisha called Lotus Blossom. We both appeared with the Mercury Players, a touring professional company, in *Juno and the Paycock*. She gained a scholarship to RADA before her sixteenth birthday; a truly talented actress who later appeared in *Z Cars*. I found the theatre so enthralling that I joined the Group Theatre in Belfast, an amazing company at the time with Colin Blakely, Jimmy Ellis, Maurice O'Callaghan, J.G. Devlin and Lilly Begley. I had persuaded the artistic director, Harold Goldblatt, that I had a wealth of experience and possessed a talent not to be missed. That year we staged the British premier of *Summer of the Seventeenth Doll* about rough Australian cane-cutters.

The pay was so poor that I slept in the theatre workroom, wrapped in discarded main tab curtains. The place smelt of glue and powdered paint, as that was where we built and painted scenery. Preparing for one of the plays, I had the good fortune to meet an extraordinary character called George Galway McCann, who had been drafted in to help with the scenery. George was a renowned sculptor who had been taught by Henry Moore in the

Royal Academy in 1932 after graduating from Belfast. A few years before we met he had exhibited with Moore, Hepworth and Epstein. By coincidence he had taught my uncle James in Armagh Royal School. George was not only a sculptor but also a painter, author, broadcaster and lecturer in art. A tall, gaunt figure with a shapeless, long overcoat and a voice rough-cast with the cigarettes which were rarely out of his mouth, he shambled into the theatre at noon and announced that it was time for lunch.

He took pity on my accommodation and offered me temporary space on his floor at 23 Botanic Avenue. His wife, Mercy Hunter, also a distinguished artist, did not approve, principally because George and I arrived after spending the afternoon in Lavery's Bar. In spite of that, I was allowed to stay. We seemed to live on Camembert and port wine and drift from one long lunch to the next. Mercy was a formidable lady who attempted to control her husband with limited success. He feigned his terror of her and charmed his way out of the worst affrays. Their house attracted a fascinating array of creative people, such as Dylan Thomas, Stanley Spencer and Louis MacNiece.

It was on the opening night of the Australian play that I was gifted my first truly memorable sexual experience. As it was the Irish premiere a collection of dignitaries was invited and a copious amount of free champagne was supplied. One of the people helping to paint the scenery was an art student called Evelyn who, after the show and our odd glass of champagne, invited me to a party with the set designer Lewis Logan. We spent the night together at his flat. It was one of those occasions where things just happened, neither making any demands on the other or harbouring any expectations. Evelyn was an exceptionally talented artist, just finishing in college. We had three days together before she left for London and fame.

I wrote this after she left, calling it 'Belfast':

> I remember where we were
> The ripples on the river in the night,
> The murmur of the city as it slept
> And, in the gasworks yard, an engine spouting fire.
> A ship slid past as silent as a snake
> Shimmering in its wake the skeletons
> Of cranes and masts and mooring wire.
> I remember too
> How selflessly you gave yourself,
> Searching my eyes for any signs of pain
> As if we had drunk hemlock
> And were content to sleep
> And never wake again.

Many years later I met Evelyn again in Scotland. She could not recall the encounter. My performance clearly had not impressed.

Through the Group I met Henry Lynch-Robinson, who was designing a set for the Grand Opera Society and asked me to help. We painted the enormous flats behind the screen of a cinema where there were flies and a gallery. I can still recite dialogue from *The Joker is Wild* and *Eighty Days around the World* which we saw back-to-front day after day. I was given the job of stage manager for *Carmen* and *Rigoletto*, a task for which I was singularly unqualified. However, the shows went on without any obvious disasters. I think it was Henry's influence that secured the position, as it did indeed for the next adventure.

Dublin. What a breath of fresh air! A long way from the oppressive, bigoted world of the Black North. A city vibrant with culture and creativity, a metropolis in which people could argue for the intellectual exercise without recrimination. A beautiful Georgian city beetling with bicycles. There was, however, a shadow over it. Signs of extreme poverty were still evident then, with women, their bairns wrapped in their shawls, begging at the stations. Children with rickets and eye infections. Long before the Celtic Tiger. Homosexuality was illegal, of course, but because I had been introduced to the city by Henry who was gay, everyone assumed I had the same preference and I moved in a secret underworld of gay men meeting together in hotels and private clubs. Promiscuity was uncommon then, and many of the relationships had lasted for decades. These were men of influence and status – lawyers, doctors, politicians. Sad, really, that they should have been so afraid.

Henry had secured me a position as stage manager in the Gate Theatre for a production of Congreve's *The Way of the World*. Strange that I should have been in the same theatre as my mother had been before the war, and I met some of the actors with whom she had appeared – Micheal MacLiammoir, Hylton Edwards and Shelagh Richards. Micheal and Hylton had just parted then, Hylton having discovered a young actor called Paddy Bedford. A regular visitor to our rehearsals was Brendan Behan – he of the very fierce wee wife who was trying fruitlessly to contain his drinking. *The Way of the World* produced some magnificent performances – Aidan Grenell as one of the fops, Dermot Tuohy as the ribald country squire and Shelagh Richards as the aged but appropriately named Lady Wishfort. I saw Dermot during rehearsals as Captain Cat in *Under Milk Wood*, a moving performance that I will never forget.

While I was in Dublin the Group Theatre virtually collapsed. The company was keen to stage a new play by Gerald McLarnon called *The Bonefire*. Set in Belfast, it dealt with the reality of sectarian strife in the city. The timid Board of Governors, fearful that the play might offend certain sections of the community, refused to stage it. Furious, Jimmy Ellis and the cast presented it themselves in the Grand Opera House in August 1958. It sold out and I was back in time to see it. It was a powerful play set on the night before the twelfth of July with mob violence, rhythmic chanting, primitive drumbeats and sensational effects such as twin pillars of orange fire bursting from the stage. Colin Blakely's brilliant portrayal of a young Catholic street fighter stunned the house into silence and inspired me to return to Dublin where there was more work available.

The Group was clearly in trouble. Harold Goldblatt had resigned and worse was to follow. Learning nothing from *The Bonefire* episode, the Board of Governors repeated their error the following year with Sam Thompson's *Over the Bridge*, once again refusing to risk controversy, and once again Jimmy and the cast took the play to the Empire Theatre to packed houses. A new company, Ulster Bridge Productions, was formed and the writing was on the wall for the Group.

8

That time in Dublin is a bit of a blur, as I seem to have spent many evenings in hostelries like Davy Byrne's and Neary's. It was under the influence of alcohol that I had my first unpleasant sexual experience. A shabby room above a café called the Dog and Waffle. An iron bedstead, sagging in the middle, a single cane chair, a chest of drawers with broken handles, a threadbare mat on the linoleum floor and frayed curtains. In the bathroom a toilet with a cracked Bakelite seat and an antique bath stained green beneath the leaking tap. Behind the building a slaughterhouse and stockyard. The cattle to be killed roared through the night but, just before dawn when the slaughter commences, an uncanny silence settles over the pens. That silence was more disturbing than the noise. Still, the room was cheap at £2. 19 shillings a week.

He was another actor, handsome, perfidious, promiscuous. When I returned to the room after an evening in Davy Byrne's he came with me. We were both dizzy with drink. Rape is an emotive term, evocative of violence, brutality, pain and lust. In many cases that portrayal is true but in some instances the experience may be less extreme. What follows, though, is probably universal. The shame, self-loathing, disgust and dread – the dread of the act becoming public knowledge. The shame is not a dark vortex spinning downward but a fire, a blaze of indescribable heat, white-hot in the core, an explosion of molten lava, ignited by the nauseous memory, unquenchable. An uncontainable flow, cremating, consuming, vaporising.

I left the Dog and Waffle in the dawn, walking along the Liffey to cool the furnace in my head. The dark, cold water was so inviting, a healing liniment. Flowing under the bridge, calm, oblivious. Imagine it extinguishing the coals, closing over them, flowing, caressing, soothing, cleansing. Standing on the bridge, fingers trembling on the parapet, limbs twitching, hesitating, one second poised to jump, the next sagging in fear. Wanting it to end yet frightened of the pain, gasping, breathing water. If you could peel off the odious person, drown it in the river and assume a new one, fresh, pristine, unsullied; but living meant imprisonment, a life sentence within the flawed carapace of the person I was. In the end cowardice helped me to choose but it was the beginning of disintegration.

I went to live with Maurice O'Brien in Monkstown. A gentle, generous and cultured Dubliner, Maurice seemed to sense that I was hurting. He was one of the gay community but never made any advances. He had been a star when he was young, the juvenile lead whom every producer tried to entice into his cast. Extraordinarily handsome, beautiful even, he was Dublin's answer to Douglas Fairbanks. Yet tragedy struck. One side of his face became paralysed and sagged, leaving him with a twisted mouth, distorted speech and a half-closed eye. He never walked on a stage again. His kindness helped to heal.

I do have fond memories of the theatre in Dublin. I fell in love with Pauline Delaney, an actress in the Globe Theatre, but she was married to Norman Rodway so the infatuation came to nothing. Besides, everyone fell in love with her. A kind, effervescent, intelligent lady with a musical Dublin brogue, she was irresistible. The little Globe Theatre in Dun Laoghaire was difficult to find. Situated above a gas showroom, the foyer was decorated with cookers, heaters and gas advertisements. Yet, upstairs, the cast staged some remarkable shows such as Isherwood's *I am a Camera*. Godfrey Quigley, who went on to star in *Educating Rita* and *The Clockwork Orange*, founded the Globe and directed the plays which I saw there during rehearsals in the Gate. They were a great company.

I spent an evening with Christopher Casson in Herbert Street and still remember vividly his recitation of the Yeats poem 'The Withering of the Boughs' accompanying himself on the harp. Truly magical. Christopher had worked in the Gate when my mother was there and, as she carried a great affection for him, she insisted that I should visit him in Dublin and bring back a description. I was able to tell her that he remembered her fondly.

After *The Way of the World* I found my way home. A touring company called the Mercury Players were in the town and I charmed my way into a small part in *Juno and the Paycock*. My sister, Mary, who had been given her scholarship to RADA, also had a part. She was not sixteen at the time. One of the company, Ronnie Wilkinson, was later to become her husband. He was a superb actor with an impressive tenor voice. Having alopecia, he could accomplish remarkable transformations to his appearance with stage make-up and wigs.

It was through him that I embarked on the next adventure. Anew McMaster's theatre company started many actors and playwrights on their careers. Harold Pinter, Peter O'Toole, Henry Woolf served their time with Mac, taking plays to different parts of Ireland. Mac, one of the old actor managers with one of the most versatile voices that I have heard, played the leading roles – even the juvenile leads! He being familiar with the parts, rehearsal time in Dublin was cut to a minimum and those of us new to scripts had to learn the parts virtually overnight. We toured with six plays, remaining a week in each place. In February 1959, for example, we staged *As You Like It*, *Macbeth*, *Rebecca*, *Jane Eyre*, *The Ideal Husband* and *Dear Delinquent* in Kilkenny, then moved on to Carlow. It was a truly taxing but invaluable experience, carrying all our own scenery, costumes, lighting and major props. We used to sell raffle tickets in the interval for the 'Irish Actors' Benevolent Fund', a completely fictitious charity which provided drinking money after the show.

That was Mac's last tour I believe. We finished in Limerick and I remember Mac and his diminutive wife hurrying back to Dublin where their house had been on fire. He was desperately keen to reassure himself that a cigarette case given to him by Ivor Novello had been saved from the flames. Ronnie and I were left destitute in Limerick and hitch-hiked back to Dublin. My mother sent us the fare back to Bangor by telegram.

It was at this point that I had a 'nervous breakdown'. I lost the plot. No idea who I was. The fruitless search to find someone to rescue you from that morass, a hand to pull you out as you sink ever deeper into the quagmire, is truly terrifying. You sprint through the streets trying to escape from a nameless, shapeless fear. The nights are spent trying to stay awake, fearful of the demons which lurk in the caverns of sleep. Lying on the floor singing 'Wait till the sun shines Nelly',waiting for the doctor with his needle to bring oblivion. Speaking to family, friends, doctors, psychiatrists, ministers, hoping that someone will calm the storm, banish the terror, piece you together, heal the wounds. No-one. The little blue pill the only answer. The pill that gets you through the night, dulls the pain, mothballs the mind.

It was Iona that saved me from self-destruction. The small island in the Inner Hebrides, the island of Columba, of white sand and azure seas, a 'thin place' where the past, present and future meet, where the eternal is just beneath the surface. For some reason I felt that I would find peace there and wrote to the leader of the Iona Community, George MacLeod, asking if I could visit. He replied that the accommodation was fully booked. I went anyway. George was a remarkable man. Decorated with an MC in World War One, he became a pacifist and an ardent opponent of nuclear warfare. He founded the Iona Community during the inter-war Depression not only to provide work for unemployed craftsmen but to rebuild the island's abbey and provide a centre for graduating ministers to learn to live and work together. If they joined the Community, they had to undertake work in deprived parishes or the mission fields.

From that remote island he built a dynamic team of dedicated activists which spread across the world, a diaspora which reached Africa, India, America and the slums of industrial Britain. The demands on his time were extreme, yet he found space to help shattered individuals who appeared on the island. He sat up with me for two nights running in his home to wean me off the psychiatric drugs to which I was addicted.

Iona attracted an extraordinary collection of individuals at that time, not only theologians but writers, painters, political activists, musicians, doctors – the avant-garde from all over the world. In my first winter there, when the Abbey community shrank to a small group of craftsmen, I spent a week with R.D. Laing talking far into the night about Zen Buddhism, Subud, Kahlil Gibran, yoga and of course his work in London. I also met Vinoba Bhava, a follower of Ghandi and founder of Bhoodan, a radical land-reform movement in India. Committed to non-violence, he walked round the country persuading land-lords to give up part of their estate to settle the landless poor and eventually gained more than four million acres for the move-ment. He was an old man when he visited Scotland, but the flame of his dedication still burned brilliantly.

In the summer the Community ran youth camps on the island, one of them under canvas at the north end and another in a bunkhouse in the village. The former attracted an extraordi-nary young lady as one of the staff. A student of English at St Andrews University, she possessed a natural ability to relate to young people and understand their difficulties. When a youth on the island ran amok with a knife she was the one who dealt with him, persuading him to meet the police, who had arrived on the island, and accompanying him calmly down to the ferry. George MacLeod decided that what I needed was a woman of this calibre and, after the season was over, invited her back to help in the Abbey kitchen where I was working. A seismic event in my life. A highly intelligent, athletic, blonde, blue-eyed girl sharing the sinks. Jan Gemmell.

And what a setting! The ancient, moss-clad granite walls and arches of the Abbey. The shadowed cloisters where black-hooded monks once walked. Flattened gravestones, their carvings of nameless armed warriors worn thin by the weather. The Abbey nave with its glittering schist flagstone floor leading up to the marble altar. Tall Celtic crosses intricately carved by craftsmen more than five centuries ago. And the island itself with its brilliant white sands, azure sea and carpets of wild flowers on the machair.

My first attempt at wooing was a disaster. There I was with a small group of young men seated at a table in the otherwise empty dining hall. For some reason she had to walk past us to the far end of that long, echoing hall.

'Light of my life, come and sit beside me,' I called.

'What a horrible little man!' she thought, and proceeded impassively on.

George MacLeod, however, persisted in his match-making, breezing into the kitchen in the afternoons.

'Far too nice a day for you young folk to be in here. Out you go for a walk.'

I was delighted. Jan had reservations but tolerated the intrusion.

This was the fragile beginning of a relationship that has lasted more than half a century, surviving crises which would have annihilated many weaker friendships.

9

On Iona in 1959 I discovered that hard physical labour helped me to sleep at night and gave me a new image, portraying a rugged, outdoor male in touch with the natural world – a pale precursor of Bear Grylls – and I was seen around the island clad only in a pair of shorts. My hero of the first summer there was Tom Forsyth, who later founded a community in Scoraig near Ullapool and was involved with the community purchase of Eigg. His blond hair and magnificent bronzed physique caused swooning and consternation among the young Christian ladies who visited the Holy Island, a good reason to imitate him.

This Adonis, however, did not impress Jan, so I thought it wise to assume another image. I became a poet, a move calculated to display my sensitive side. I enthralled some elderly ladies so effectively that they paid for the publication of a book of verse. I don't think Jan was taken in, however, and I had to pursue her relentlessly after she left the island. By an extraordinary stroke of luck my sister had moved to St Andrews where Jan was a student. Mary had married Ronnie Wilkinson who was working in the Byre Theatre there and so I had a place to stay while courting Miss Gemmell.

By that time I had left Iona to live in Iona Community House in Glasgow, a tall eighteenth-century building overlooking the Clyde. Like Iona, it was a fascinating centre. On the ground floor, opening on to Clyde Street and the suspension bridge, there was a restaurant which served the most eclectic group of people in the city – bus drivers and conductors, wine drinkers from the hostels, office workers, art students, Christian youth workers and political activists. At night the windowless basement vibrated with visceral music from folk to rock and sweated with the steam from the mass of swaying dancers. The first floor had meeting rooms where serious activists plotted revolution or planned radical reformation of the Church. The air was alive with Marx, Ouspensky, Gurdjieff, Tao Te Ching, Christmas Humphreys, Camus, Buber, C.S. Lewis. It was a meeting place for the avant-garde. Alasdair Gray, who was work-ing on a vast mural, used to drop in and Tom Buchan, author of the *Great Northern Welly Boot Show* with Billy Connolly, had a room in the building.

Tom Buchan was to become a great friend, reappearing peri-odically from the wings on to the stage of my life till his tragic death in 1995. One of Scotland's leading poets of the time, he was a superb raconteur and wit with a fascinating repertoire of tales from India where he had been teaching English in Madras. Incorrigible, irrepressible, unpredictable, hilarious and danger-ously intelligent, he is sadly under-rated as a literary figure in Scotland.

'I guess I'll die unknown,' he wrote to me in 1992, 'or be talked about after my death. Who cares? I don't. But it would be nice to have a wee hoosie for my old age.'

He had been the Warden in Community House when I first met him and had attracted all kinds of anarchic groups into the building.

It was from Community House that I started climbing and developed an addiction to the high hills and wildernesses of the

Highlands. I met a draughtsman from Uddingston who used to escape from his job designing coal-cutters at Maver and Coulson to climb in what we called the 'Arrochar Alps' at weekends. We used to hitch-hike out of Glasgow on a Friday night to spend two nights in the hills. I have a vivid memory of a winter night camped in the snow just below the summit of the Cobbler. In bright moonlight we walked along the ridge at midnight, the snow glistening in the pale light and my breath freezing on my beard. The only sound in the magnificent silence was the crunching of our boots on the snow. On another occasion, we spent a night under a shelter stone on the Brack and, unable to sleep as the icy cold penetrated the primitive kapok sleeping bags, we rose and climbed a rock face in the dark.

In those days our rudimentary equipment was usually bought from ex-army stores – commando-soled boots with tricounis, anoraks from the Korean war, hemp ropes, Primus stoves. We rather despised mountaineers who appeared with shining duvet jackets and pristine boots. We were the hard men, the real mountain men, so we thought. One evening, just about dusk, when we were in a remote bothy, we saw a couple of these fashion-conscious mountaineers climbing towards our shelter. A stray cat had produced kittens in the corner and my friend lifted one of these, placed it between two pieces of bread and met the men at the door with the bread at his mouth and the kitten's tail twirling from the crust.

'Whatja want, pal?' he growled.

They didn't come in.

I slept alone in Community House on the third floor in a wide dormitory with ranks of iron bedsteads normally filled with groups on their way to Iona, and, being penniless, hitch-hiked through to St Andrews at weekends to be fed. It was at this stage that I made quite an unusual pilgrimage to England. A rather esoteric Eastern philosophy called Subud had a centre at Coombe Springs south of London and, keen to visit it, I boarded a train for London. Having no ticket and seeing the ticket collector approach, I climbed on to the roof. It was an exhilarating experience racing through the countryside with a panoramic view of the hills. Naturally I was caught and marched away ignominiously between two burly policemen at the next station to spend the night in the cells. George MacLeod of Iona paid the fine and rescued me from custody. Sadly, the adventure was reported in the press and the prospects of a successful outcome to my romantic ambitions began to fade. Jan was furious. My father's comment in the newspaper was, 'Extraordinary! Just like the Wild West.'

I returned to Iona, Jan resumed her studies, and I pestered her with a stream of letters designed to impress her with my new 'maturity'. I did persuade her to return to the island the following summer where she found work on one of the crofts. What a wonderful summer! She stayed in a tent in the stackyard and I visited at night, creeping back to the Abbey in the glistening dew and wondering if Columba's monks found similar recreation. They seem so distant now, those days of contentment and exploration. Half a century separates us from the intensity of those feelings, the senses alive to every touch and word, and only memories remain. The crescents traced by marram grass in the sand beside her hair, the ripples of the turquoise sea around her feet, her fingers curled round mine beneath the ancient cross. In her I found myself.

I secured work with the Forestry Commission in Comrie, Perthshire. The squad was a mixed bunch, one of them just out of prison, and I had digs with a wonderful lady who had four children by different fathers. The boys predicted that the next one would be born with a beard and have an Irish accent. She was a warm, voluptuous, kind lady with a great sense of humour whose only fault was her enthusiasm for providing cold mince sandwiches for my lunch. I swapped them for cheese with the ex-convict.

The work involved a great deal of draining with tools which now appear in folk museums – an enormous twin-handled spade with a heart-shaped blade called a rutter, a three-pronged fork at right angles to the handle called a hawk and a shovel. Armed with these, we cut drains along the slopes of Ben More at Crianlarich and laid out mounds for planting. We were paid on piece-work, the rates being adjusted so that, if we looked like earning too much, they were scaled down. There were constant arguments over rates which varied from 5 shillings per chain (22 yards) to 10 shillings. The ex-convict, however, never seemed to have trouble with the diminutive forester. One of the squad, known as The Bogle, always dressed in an airman's flying helmet and flying jacket and rarely spoke to anyone. Withdrawn and eccentric, he had been one of the first into Hiroshima.

It was while working in the forestry that I finally persuaded Jan to join me in a flat in Crieff. Convention at that time still insisted that her parents should be consulted so I hitched down to Ayrshire and confronted her father. Naturally he asked if I could support his daughter, and I boasted that I earned between £7 and £11 per week and that this should be enough for any sensible couple. He then asked if I had any savings to fall back on. I had £7 in my back pocket. Having hoped that his daughter would wed an architect, a lawyer or a civil engineer, he was clearly disappointed. In spite of his disapproval we were married in Beith on 4 February 1961 – a cold, dreich day with snow on the roads.

There was no honeymoon in the West Indies or the South of France but the statutory four days off in the flat. We travelled to Crieff by bus, sitting on our feet as the heating had failed, but were greatly cheered to find that Jan's ancient great aunts had left a profusion of flowers in the flat.

Not having a fortune to live on, we found that one of the local stores sold off, very cheaply, tins of food which had lost their labels, and took advantage of this. So we might have gooseberries for a main course and sausage and beans for dessert or three days of spaghetti. Our first quarrel was when, with my usual restraint, I ate two Mars bars one after the other.

I did try to obtain a forestry house at Rowardennan, spending a Friday night with Tom Buchan in his remote cottage west of Kinlochard and walking over Beinn a' Bhan to Cashel the following day. We had a splendid dinner of venison which he had killed a few days beforehand and he drove me to Comer farm in the morning. I was not to know that I would be herding Ben Lomond above Comer a few years later.

We returned briefly to Iona as I had undertaken to help with a camp run for boys from one of the Borstals. Set in a very remote salmon-fishing station at Camas on the Ross of Mull, these camps were designed to give the boys an experience of a completely different way of life and to float the idea of alternatives to their criminal habits. Some had never seen the sea. We took them out fishing for lithe and 'cuddies', and to see the fright and delight in their pale faces when they caught their first fish was amazing; and when they carried it back to camp for supper, they could not conceal their pride. One of the boys came to live with us later in Arran, moving on to work on a farm on the island. Our first foster boy.

Jan and I chose a very different way of life from that of our parents, deliberately turning our backs on 'the establishment', its controls, its values, its greed. Like many other young people in the 60s we wanted to live a more natural life, divorced from the voracious engines of materialism. We looked towards the philosophy in E.F. Schumacher's *Small Is Beautiful* and the view that people were more important than profit. We were keen to bring up children in the countryside where they would have freedom and an understanding of the natural world. The establishment saw our generation as self-indulgent, subversive and idealistic. True that few of its dreams of changing the world have been fulfilled, yet the Green movement, growth of renewable energy sources and concern for climate change are part of the legacy.

We did consider joining a Rudolf Steiner community in Botton Village near Danby in Yorkshire, a collective for young adults with Down's Syndrome, and we hitch-hiked down to visit the place. The idea of working with it had been inspired by a friendship with Carlo Piezner, the leader of a Steiner community in Ireland who was one of the most caring, creative and tranquil people I had encountered. He was indeed a whole person, and the children and staff in his care were wonderfully happy and welcoming. However, Peter Roth in Botton was a very different man – reserved, distant, suspicious. We did not take to him and we felt that many of the staff lived in this sheltered community because they themselves needed a refuge from the cruel world outside. Certainly the young people were involved in some exceptional work – glass-engraving and toy-making for Harrods, horticulture and forestry – but we felt that the ethos of the place was too exclusive for us and the staff too effete. Besides, we suddenly discovered Jan was pregnant!

From Crieff we used to visit a farming couple in Killin, the wife of whom I had charmed on Iona. They had a hill sheep farm and, weary of my complaints about the constant arguments in the forestry, she suggested that I should become a shepherd. I think she felt that a solitary occupation where there was no-one to argue with would suit my temperament. It was an excellent suggestion, but I had no dog, no knowledge, no experience and no job. Easy. Never one to be thwarted, I persuaded a minister who had a farm on Arran to employ me on his mixed farm in Blackwaterfoot. And so we moved – the first steps of a pattern of vagrancy that lasted for most of our married life.

Jan by this time was expansively pregnant and, as we lived in a small tent with a tunnel entrance, had to abandon her dignity and squeeze through the tunnel. Sadly, we had no camera. A neighbouring farmer took pity on us and offered a house and a job. And so we moved. The small farm was mainly dairy with a few sheep and pigs. Contrary to popular belief, pigs are clean animals and will leave their sleeping part of a pen clean. However, the smell of pig manure is the most virulent scent in the countryside, penetrating and permeating clothes, kitchens, bedrooms, wardrobes and suits. If you travelled by bus on a wet day, fellow passengers could tell where you were employed. Nevertheless I grew quite fond of the animals.

Our first son was born in Arran. Sadly, I was not able to be present at the birth as the hospital was on the far side of the island, and the bus service did not fit in with milking times. PB came to visit us once and inspect his first Orr grandson, who met with his approval. We were castrating pigs at the time. He seemed to enjoy the weekend on the farm, a relief perhaps from the excesses of life in London. In a sense he envied the apparent simplicity of the life we had chosen.

Dairy work in those days was a form of slavery, a monotonous routine repeated day after day, month after month. No such luxury as relief milkers then. Up at 5.30 every day into the byre and, in the summer, working at hay or harvest till dusk. Cold, dark mornings in the winter and long, hard days in the summer. The machine milking was fairly primitive, with the compressed air pipes round the byre above the cattle driving suction clusters which drew the milk out of the teats into a metal churn – like four bovine vibrators. After winter milking there was always other work – cutting kale, lifting turnips, bruising oats, fencing, splitting firewood. The travelling mill came round to thresh the corn stacks, separating the grain from the straw. A real social event, as workers from neighbouring farms came to help, providing a little light relief in a tedious timetable. There was little chance of learning much about sheep-herding on the farm. And so we moved.

I had been opening drains for a hill farmer further up the valley when he offered me a job as a shepherd, and a house.

'But I've no dog,' I confessed.

'You can get a dog.'

When I told other workers that I was going to work for Johnnie MacAllister, their comments were unanimous.

'God, don't work for him, crabbit wee man, and he'll work you to death.'

I made up my own mind and took the job. Johnnie was the best employer I encountered. A wee man with a lame leg, he had worked as a stockman in the frozen north of Canada, guarding sheep from the wolves and sledging hay across ice-covered rivers. He had a vision of his farm as it could be, and bit by bit transformed it from bracken and rushes to fertile pasture. He had a feeling for the land like few others. He fought with it, nurtured it, coaxed it, cursed it. On one occasion, after the calf sales, he had some extra cash and the family wanted a car. Johnnie bought a small crawler tractor to reclaim the high ground. I understood his passion and learned much from him.

10

It was at this time that my sister in London, having had two children, then produced twins and left her husband. She wrote to Jan and asked her to go down and help Ronnie, her husband, with the two left behind. Right in the middle of lambing, but Jan had to go. Ronnie had given up the precarious profession of acting to take a secure position as a Studio Manager with the BBC, but this sacrifice was not enough to heal Mary's growing dissatisfaction. She had been far too young for a family and felt deprived of her youth. She went to live with Michael Forrest who was in *Z Cars* at the time and earning a good income. Ronnie never really recovered from the loss.

It was through him that I met a folk-singer who was to become one of our closest friends. Ronnie was working on the *Tonight* programme on which Robin Hall and Jimmie Macgregor made regular appearances and brought Scottish folksong to the notice of TV audiences. When the duo were performing in Arran they came to stay with us in Shedock, and from that visit emerged the friendship. The duo rarely get enough credit for the stimulus they gave to the Scottish folk revival of the 1960s as the purists claim that they prostituted the art by commercialisation. Without them, however, the revival might have been confined to small groups of hairy purists whining monotonous ballads with one hand behind an ear.

Robin had a magnificent tenor voice (listen to 'O Sinner Man') and Jimmie had an acute sense of harmony and originality. Sadly, Robin died alone as an alcoholic but Jimmie soldiered on, hosting popular radio and TV programmes, writing, singing and promoting Scottish music. Today his one-man shows with hilarious stories and traditional songs provide a superb evening's entertainment. Nearing 90 now, he is still one of the finest ambassadors for Scottish culture.

We escaped from the island occasionally to get a whiff of civilisation, attending a Pete Seeger concert in Glasgow and the Edinbugh Folk Festival. The latter was held in the YMCA and included traditional singers like Jimmy MacBeath, Jeannie Robertson and Willie Scott, the 'singing shepherd'. The organisers had also managed to attract musicians like Josh MacRae, Matt McGinn and young Archie Fisher. I remember an early performance of the original Corries with Paddy Bell in the Roy Guest's Howff in Edinburgh, their repertoire at that time consisting largely of Clancy Brothers' material and Robin and Jimmie's songs.

We used to visit our friends in Abbotsford Place in the Gorbals who were working for the Iona Gorbals Group with Geoff Shaw, Walter Fyffe and and John Jardine. The Group ran as a small community, doing what it could to alleviate the worst effects of oppressive poverty and deprivation in the area. Geoff later became the first Convener of the mammoth and cumbersome Strathclyde Region. One of the group, a folksong enthusiast, had a great collection of records, including EPs of the Galliards, Isabel Sutherland and Robin Hall, from which Jan and I learnt songs to sing at ceilidhs on Arran. We were known as the poor man's Nina and Frederick.

Back on the farm I managed to procure a superb working dog called Mandy after Mandy Rice-Davies. She was almost pure white (the dog that is, not the lady) and became a 'one man' dog, refusing to work for anyone else. She had two major faults. She could not be seen in the snow and had an insatiable appetite for stinking 'braxy' – the meat off carcasses on the hill.

The Dog's Eye View

See me? Ah'm swift and sleek,
Oot on the hill a wee white streak,
Swifter 'n a' they stupit sheep.
An' him doon there? He bawls and wheeps,
Big hob buits stuck tae his feet,
Waves his stick with the lambin' cleek,
He cannae rin like me, see?

He feeds me, tho', wi' maize an' meat
An' gies me straw tae warm ma feet,
An' whiles ah get a bain tae eat.
When ah wis wee an' just a pup,
A wee roon rompin' ba' o' fluff,
He clapped ma heid an' tugged ma ruff
An' ca'd me 'hen' then.

An' noo? Aye noo
Ah get a grunt when ah shed right
Or fetch his tupps doon tae the dyke
Or hunt the coo in for the night.
Noo when the snaws blaw in a heap

An' whirl an' bury half the sheep
Beneath a snaw wreath ten feet deep
Ah show him where tae delve an' screed
An' pu' them oot afore they're deid.
He nods but disnae clap ma heid
Nor gie me extra meat tae eat.

He cannae see me in the snaw
Ah slink awa' and slyly gnaw
Auld braxy meat frae last year's thaw,
Fer jings, the taste is awfu' sweet
O' maggot grubs an' mingin' meat,
But when ah barf it gars him greet.
It's braw blaw, tho'.

Still, he's ma man,
Ah'd leave ma pups an' stinkin' meat
Tae go wi' him aroon' his beat
An' sclim the screes that slice ma feet
For a' that.
See when Ah'm done an' past ma peak,
He'll lift me up when Ah am weak,
His faithfu' tike, his wee white streak.
He'll clap me then, ken.

Lambing cleek – crook for catching sheep.
Shed – Divide one sheep from another.
Braxy – carcass of dead sheep.
Blaw – Gypsy travellers' word for meat.

The work with Johnnie was mostly with sheep, but he had a herd of belted Galloways which had to be tested for TB. Normally quite placid, the beasts took on the character of wild bison if we tried to imprison them in a pen. Still, they had to be tested, so we managed to herd them into a stable with a small window high in the wall for light. The vet and myself were shut in to stab each one in the neck with a needle. The bull suddenly went wild, bellowing and climbing up on the backs of the cows. I turned to the vet to suggest a retreat, only to see the heels of his wellies disappearing out of the window. 'He who fights and runs away lives to fight another day.'

One summer Johnnie sent me to borrow a horse to rake the hay. I think horses and I were created under a different scheme, for we seem to have nothing in common. I arrived at the neighbouring farm and asked to borrow the mare.

'She's in the field,' the farmer replied.

'How do I get her?'

'Take that wee pail of nuts and, when she bends down, catch her by the forelock, bring her up here and I'll yoke her.'

In the field the great Clydesdale mare sauntered over and dipped her muzzle in the pail as predicted. I grabbed her forelock but she just stood up and I was left hanging helplessly in the air. Humiliated, I had to get help and made the morning memorable for the neighbours. Still, I did learn to yoke and handle the mare and spent some contented afternoons sitting on the horse rake as she plodded along the rows in the sun.

I bought another dog, Nell, who developed one very annoying habit. At the march on top of the hill there was a series of peat haggs where the gulls nested every spring. Once when I was gathering sheep out there the gulls, infuriated by our invasion of their site, viciously attacked Nell who fled home. After that, if ever I appeared to be heading for the march, she turned tail and sped back to her kennel. Our sheep often strayed across the march, so I had to rely on the white dog. Our neighbour over the hill in Glenscorrodale was young Willie McConnell, whose son Jack was to become First Minister and Lord Glenscorrodale.

One of the tasks before the summer shearing was to look for sheep on their backs. Sometimes a ewe would roll on her back to scratch an itch, only to find that, with the weight of her fleece, she could not rise again. Gradually her stomach would fill with gas and she would be asphyxiated or, more often, the black-backed gulls would tear her entrails from her distended gut and leave her to die. It was a miserable sight to find the beast dead and her intestines spread around the heather like white ribbons. It prompted an irrational hatred of the voracious birds with their yellow beaks. They would feast on the eyes of a living ewe or the tongue of a lamb stuck out at birth with its head protruding from its mother's back end.

One of the hardest winters of my years herding came in February 1963, when a snow storm swept in from the east. It covered the hills so quickly that we had not enough time to gather in the ewes from the distant hefts. I went out in the blizzard to retrieve some of them but it became a complete white-out and I couldn't recognise the landmarks on the hill – an area of which I thought I knew every outcrop. As daylight faded I had to turn back, trudging through knee-deep drifts and searching for the hill dyke. It was nowhere to be seen. Eventually, in the dusk, I found a fence, only to discover I had come down two miles from where I thought I was. Even in the fields the storm wreaked havoc. There was a deep gully in one of them with a fence across the dip. Some wedder hoggs wintering there moved into the gully for shelter. Those nearest the fence were soon covered in snow and the ones behind them moved in on top of them. They too were covered and the next lot moved in. They were five layers deep in the morning, the bottom layers smothered to death.

Out on the hill we spent days looking for buried ewes, often located in the drifts by a small yellow hole where the beast's breath had melted the snow above it. We rescued many of them, but some perished before we could reach them. One old ewe survived under a heather bank for three weeks and reared a good lamb in the spring. In some respects we were fortunate, losing less than three score of the flock. A flockmaster in Kintyre lost two hundred that winter.

After the snow came a spell of freezing weather. Our water supply froze but I was able to fetch water from a burn below the house. The track down to the main road was filled with a drift which covered the five-bar gate. When that froze we were marooned and we were not alone. A travelling drapery salesman from Pakistan, who stayed with us when he was in the area, had parked his car at the house so he had to wait for the thaw. I discovered that we were using a great deal of water. The more I carried from the burn, staggering under the weight of a baby bath, the faster it disappeared. Eventually I discovered that our guest, adhering strictly to his Muslim practices, was washing thoroughly twice a day.

'Chima,' I said, 'You know that we respect your faith and your need to wash in an infidel's house, but please carry your own water.'

He remained a great friend and taught us to make authentic curries, one of the few benefits of the storm.

11

Keen to get more experience, I found a job with one of the top Blackface tup (ram) breeders in Scotland. And so we moved again. This time to Lanarkshire. I finished with Johnnie the day after J.F. Kennedy was shot on 22 November 1963, an assassination which shocked the world and killed the hopes of a generation. I was sorry to leave Johnnie, who swore that, if I left, he would never get another man, a pledge that he kept till he died. Robert Hamilton of South Cobbinshaw had a farm at Handaxwood with a brand-new house near Breich. It was a strange herding as the hill ground was bisected by a main road and pitted with shale bings and the tunnels of a sand mine. Not exactly rural.

The previous shepherd had been a dedicated stocksman, rising early every day before five to move the sheep off the main road. Although it was tiresome, I felt I had to follow his example. However, he had confined his duties strictly to the sheep, so fences and dykes had fallen into disrepair. I spent much of the winter rebuilding the drystone march dyke to keep the neighbour's ewes off the hill. At the same time Hamilton employed a drainer to open out the hill drains and repair the small sheep bridges. These single men, working as drainers, mole-catchers and rabbit-catchers were a feature of farming then. Living their own isolated lives, they seemed to turn their backs on contact with others. This one did join us for tea-breaks occasionally and approved of the repairs to the march dyke.

It was in Handaxwood that our first daughter was born. Nothing unusual in a birth, some might say. Yet the delivery was far from conventional. I had been out in the fank clipping the tups' feet and smearing the cloven hooves with brown ointment to deal with their foot rot when I was called to the bedroom. Jan was in the final stages of labour and about to give birth. I delivered Kate clad in overalls and with hands ingrained with foot-rot paste. It was a fast, easy birth in an atmosphere of calm and warm intimacy, an environment which we think gave the baby an unusual contentment. She never cried.

Robert Hamilton was a first-class employer but there was a problem with Breich. It was a cold, bleak place and from the hill I could see the snow-topped high hills in the north. I yearned to be back there. It was at this point that I encountered Tom Forsyth again. He had married Ray Soper, the niece of the 'Red Dean', and had been working in New Harmony, Indiana, with a community there not dissimilar to the one on Iona. Returning to Scotland, they had decided to settle on the inaccessible peninsula of Scoraig near Ullapool and start a community there. Tom suggested that, with my experience with livestock, I should join them. Fired with enthusiasm, I drove north to Badluchrach, crossed Loch Broom with Tom in his dinghy (there is no road into Scoraig) and walked round his new kingdom. Most of the original croft houses were deserted and in ruins, and the land sadly neglected with rashes growing in the rigs and fences collapsed. However, some intrepid incomers had already settled there. A salmon fisherman called Allan Bush lived near the jetty and worked the salmon bag nets, and two ex-servicemen, Bridger and Gosling, had settled on a neighbouring croft. I was not sure how these settlers would react to the prospect of a community. Tom, who had trained in the Botanic Gardens, could claim to be a horticulturalist but neither a stocksman nor farmer, so he was keen for me to join him and build up the sheep stock. One deserted house was intact and he had earmarked that for himself. I walked across to the north side of the peninsula to view the building he had chosen for us. It was in a magnificent setting with a view across to the Summer Isles and Achiltibuie, but it was nothing more than a heap of stones. The dream of an idyllic crofting life shattered. I returned to Breich – a wise decision as it turned out later.

Nevertheless I longed for the high hills and so we moved. Pure self-indulgence on my part. We moved to the Isle of Mull, a memorable flit. In Oban we loaded all our belongings on to a fishing boat and, as it was a calm, sunny day, we sat in our armchairs on the deck as we crossed the Sound of Mull to Craignure. There was no car ferry then and our A35 van had to follow later on a cargo boat after being slung in a net and hoisted by derrick onto the deck. The skipper for our flit was Hugh Carmichael, a seaman who had joined the Royal Navy on the outbreak of World War Two only to spend the war in a Japanese POW camp. When he returned to the island his mother failed to recognise him. But he had survived and retained the imperturbable patience and forbearance that had seen him through the horrors. His casual approach to every situation, however, infuriated his wife Josie, a handsome actress with the tempestuous nature frequently found in the species. They became lifelong friends of ours.

On Mull I herded Dun Da Ghaoithe and Beinn Bhearnach, the first hills seen from the ferry. The estate was owned by Colonel Miller but managed by a dour, irascible Highlander from the island of Muck with whom I quickly quarrelled, an irrational tendency of mine, inevitably, I maintained, provoked by employers. And so we moved.

We were there for only a few months and moved to an uninhabited island on the west of Mull called Erraid. The island features in R.L. Stevenson's *Kidnapped* as the place where David Balfour was shipwrecked. Stevenson's father had been the engineer building the lighthouse off Mull in 1867 and the row of granite houses on Erraid were erected at that time. We lived in one of these where we had an extensive bathroom, an imposing bath with taps but neither running water nor drainage. There was no electricity and the chemical toilet was emptied off the pier. The owner had promised to train us as silversmiths to revive the hallmark of the island but, once we were there, the pledge was forgotten, as was his memory over our wages which appeared less frequently as the months passed. We managed to survive by fishing for saithe and laying lobster creels. Our creels, however, were frequently raided by the passing fishing boats. Later in the year, when I was taking the lambs to market in Oban, I complained about the vanishing wages to the manager of another estate.

'Come and work for us,' he said, 'I'll give you a house and a decent wage. Erraid is no place for a man with a family.'

And so we moved. Erraid is not really an island as the Sound dries at low water during spring tides, so we were able to load a tractor and trailer and flit across the sand to Glenforsa near Salen on Mull. This was a good move, as the manager, Angus MacGillivray, was a superb stocksman, dedicated to his management of the Department of Agriculture Estate. I learnt a great deal from him and his staff. I think there were about 4,000 Blackface ewes on the hills which stretched from Salen to Glen More and a staff of five shepherds and two cattlemen.

At Glenforsa we were introduced to a tricky new technology. Shearing by hand had been the accepted method of stripping the sheep of their wool for centuries, a fairly leisurely activity with hours of scurrilous gossip and banter. Some men clipped on stools with their backs against a dyke and pipes in their jaws. All that was suddenly transformed as machine-shearing appeared among us. Instructors came to teach us the Australian Bowen technique. As the cutting handpiece was driven by a cable from the engine, the main skill was in working the sheep around the cable. The youngsters among us picked up the technique reasonably quickly, but the older men couldn't adapt and were seen battling with the cables like snake-wrestlers or splayed out on the floor with a sheep in one hand and the handpiece in the other. The machines of course encouraged competition with the hand-shears and generally won. However, one shepherd on Mull, who could clip with both hands on a stool, could finish milk ewes faster than the machine-shearers. The machines, nevertheless, took over.

Our second son was born in Glenforsa. Not the easy, carefree birth of Kate but a frantic, blood-soaked affair in which the baby was thrown aside into a cot while the midwife panicked over an adherent placenta and caused a major haemorrhage – not helpful when there was no suitable blood on the island. The woman was so distraught that we asked her to leave and I was left with a syringe of ergot to inject when necessary. Jamie was a troubled baby, a condition which we still attribute to the crisis.

In our spare time we became involved in a drama group with Barrie and Marianne Hesketh who had just moved to the island. Having staged a couple of plays, Barrie and Marianne considered forming a professional theatre group and asked Josie Carmichael and myself if we would join. Josie had long years of experience as an actress in weekly rep before coming to the island, and I had a taste of the stage in Ireland. Both of us, however, felt we couldn't take the risk, so Barrie and Marianne went ahead on their own and formed the Little Theatre in Dervaig, which gained a nationwide reputation for its productions.

I herded Ishriff on the south west side of Ben Talla in Glenmore. On one occasion I was high out on the ridge with the head shepherd, Johnnie Miller, watching the other men gathering the sheep on the far side of the glen. We noticed that some of the flock on that side were escaping so I sent my white dog right down the side of Ben Talla, across the glen and up Ben Bhearnach to foil the bid for freedom. Johnnie, a man of few words, was impressed.

'Aye,' he said, 'pity the man is not as good as the dog.'

It was my job to drive the Land Rover round in the early morning to pick up the other men, leaving in the summer about 5.30. One morning – and only one – I slept in and woke to hear the Land Rover under the second-storey bedroom window and the unmistakeable whine of Johnnie's voice, 'Aye. She must have been good last night, Willie.'

A randy old bachelor.

One of the more unpleasant tasks was skinning dead sheep below Duart Castle. The Department, always keen to save every penny, saved the sheep skins and sent them off for processing. Some of our young sheep (hoggs) were wintered on the grazing round the Castle and I was put in charge of them. There is a saying that it is a horse's job to work, a cow's job to give milk and a sheep's job to live. Those hoggs failed in their task with monotonous regularity. There is nothing more difficult than skinning a green, stinking sheep on a freezing cold morning with fingers numb with the cold.

At that time there was talk of splitting up Glenforsa and offering the different parts to young shepherds as tenants. Angus hinted that my herding at Ishriff would make a great tenancy and, in anticipation of this, I left the Department and started out on my own, offering gathering, shearing, fencing, draining around the island – the first contract shearer on Mull. And so we moved! Took a lease of a small house near Tobermory. Unfortunately most of the work on offer was at the other end of the island, apart from a lambing contract which was in Lanarkshire! As it turned out Glenforsa was not split for some ten years.

The lambing was on a farm on the Lang Whang with Robert Hamilton's brother and brought in the princely sum of £100 for the four weeks. I stayed with the shepherd in charge, Bill Brown, who patiently taught me his way of herding his flock. What I remember most is the hard-boiled eggs. Every morning, before we left for the hill, Bill put two eggs in front of me as fortification for the long walk to the marches. Instead of counting the days left to the end of lambing, I counted the eggs. 'Only twelve hard-boiled eggs to go!' The weather was dire while I was there, blowing snow from the east for a fortnight and cold rain from the west.

I was glad to get home.

While I was there my grandmother, to whom I owed so much, died. Having committed myself to the lambing, I could not leave Bill on his own and decided not to attend the funeral in Ireland. She was buried in Carnlough not far from her mother, Kate Story. Her husband, daughter and son have since joined her there. The little cemetery is rattling with the bones of Orrs.

Our second daughter was born while we lived in Tobermory, Jan having to cross to Oban for the occasion after Jamie's dismal birth. Once again I missed the birth, having to gather and clip sheep on contract for Colonel Millar in Torosay. I had just bought a superb hunting dog called Fly and, after the gathering, I asked the manager for a secure place to keep her during the clipping. He indicated a loose-box for cattle in the yard but failed to remember that he had placed rat poison in the corner. I'm glad I did not see her die.

That was the year of the seamen's strike so we were marooned on the island. Inconvenient perhaps but also an opportunity for cunning entrepreneurs. At the time, Tawse of Aberdeen was building a new road through the Ross of Mull and advertised for a contractor to fence the sides of the new road. Knowing that there would be little chance of competition because of the strike, I submitted an inflated price and, to my astonishment, was awarded the contract. The first part of the work was to build a new sheep fank and, by good fortune, I was able to persuade a friend, who was also marooned and an experienced builder, to help. Tawse provided a caravan for him and his wife and daughter and we passed an idyllic couple of months on the Ross, erecting the fank in a casual and most lucrative manner. A memorable summer.

While I was self-employed and hoping for a holding of our own, the Highlands and Islands Enterprise Board was formed in 1965. Although its compulsory purchase powers were severely limited and it was largely controlled from Westminster, its introduction raised the hopes of many of us on Mull. The hopes were shattered the following year. The Board sent two officials to the island to clarify its role and plans for the future. At a packed meeting one of them – I think it was John Robertson – told those of us in farming, 'Do your sums. If you can't make it pay, leave.' I paraphrase but that was the substance of the advice. The hall erupted and the men were lucky to have escaped through the back door unscathed. Those rash words created so much outrage that the chairman of the Board, Professor Grieve, had to come to Tobermory a few months later in an attempt to calm the natives. For many years afterwards most of us on the island regarded the Board with suspicion and contempt. Our disillusion was confirmed when the Board's promised survey of land use on Mull failed to appear.

When a report on the island finally was published in 1973 it admitted:

Despite the survey, its recommendations, the discussions which have surrounded it and all the incentives which the board can offer to development projects, the island still provides many examples of communities and land suffering at the hands of owners whose goals and policies are in conflict with the needs and desires of the community.

12

We did eventually take a tenancy. It's the dream of every young shepherd to have a place of his or her own so we took the grazing of a hill in Glen More. And so we moved. Moved to an isolated cottage in the glen where the stags came down to the back door in the winter and the salmon spawned in the river. Idyllic? In some ways, but the cottage had no electricity and at first we had to wear oilskins to wash the dishes in wet weather because of the leaks. No washing machine and three children in nappies (one muslin, one towelling and one pair plastic pants).

While in Glen More I acquired another working dog called Roy. He belonged to a young city gent who, in spite of utter ignorance of farming or the countryside, had taken over the management of a neighbouring sheep farm from an ancient aunt. He had purchased Roy but, finding that he would not work for him, had shut him in a shed no bigger than two metres square which had been an outside toilet. Incarcerated there for weeks, the excrement piled up beneath him till it was half a metre deep. The ancient aunt stopped me one day and pleaded with me to take Roy, as her nephew was going to shoot him,

'Please, please, take him. He's such a nice wee dog and I'm sure he'll work for you. The man hasn't a clue what he's doing.'

'Alright, I'll take him but, if he doesn't work, I'll have to have him put down. I've two other dogs and can't afford to feed another.'

So Roy came to us in June and, by September, I took two hundred ewes and lambs through the streets of Oban with him. He turned out to be a splendid dog and, although I often swore at him on the hill – 'black bastard of hell' being the usual form of address – I remember him with great affection and admiration.

The small sheep stock did not provide a living so I continued contracting. One of the hill farms with which I worked was in Lochbuie owned by Mrs Sassoon, Siegfried's widow. I mentioned to her one day in the fank that I had read all his war poems and remembered lines from 'Everyone Sang':

> Everyone's voice was suddenly lifted,
> And beauty came like the setting sun.
> My heart was shaken with tears; and horror
> Drifted away . . . O but every one
> Was a bird; and the song was wordless; the singing will
>   never be done.

Every Christmas after that she sent us a bottle of whisky. Her son, George, and his wife became friends of ours for a while. I remember he spoke fluent Serbo-Croat and listened to broadcasts from Yugoslavia on amateur radio in Lochbuie. We often wondered if he worked for British Intelligence.

While we were in Craig I encountered Tom Buchan again. A brief meeting but a renewal, He had just married an actress called Alice Farley and they were heading for Iona on the single track through Pennyghael when a slight error of judgement (or something of that nature) sent the car into a ditch. Fortunately

Herbert Hughes

Frederick Patrick Hughes

Percy Story, Evelyn Story and George Story

PB in 1938

Ulster's Solemn League and Covenant, signed by William Robert Macaulay Orr in 1912

PB with the Orr family, Reverend William Orr, Jean, Evelyn and Katherine Orr

PB in his regalia as Grand Master of the Orange Lodge

PB on a banner in an Orange parade, Liverpool

PB and Brian Faulkner

PB with Terence O'Neill and George Brown

PB and Willie Orr, 1941

Willie, centre with bat, with the Garth House cricket team, 1954

Willie while in the Group Theatre, Belfast

Willie in Arran, 1961

Willie and his dog

I was passing and towed them back to the road. Alice, elegantly dressed and wearing high heels, seemed completely out of place, her city image distinctly incongruous, and not the kind of woman I expected to find with Tom. Nevertheless he was clearly very fond of her. Yet, when he came to stay with us some years later, she had left him for Tom Forsyth.

We were offered the tenancy of a farm on the Ross of Mull which had a comfortable house and good arable. Overlooking Loch Assapol and the hills of Scoor, it was a beautiful setting, Although its 700 acres was a large holding, the stock on it was so small that it was granted 'like status' to that of a croft and therefore was eligible for more generous crofting grants. In April 1967, I gathered four score ewes off the hill in Glen More and walked them by road to Saorphin. In those days when one took over a settled sheep stock part of the value lay in 'acclimatisation', which indicated that, through prolonged exposure to local diseases, the ewes had a natural resistance to infection. The distance between Glen More and Saorphin was about ten miles but our sheep from the glen died like flies on the new pasture in the late spring. Learning the hard way. Fortunately Saorphin had 70 acclimatised breeding ewes which survived. Still, we carried on with the work, planting a field of potatoes and one of oats, and 140 of the sheep survived. I still had to work away from the farm gathering, shearing and fencing for £8 an hour. Unfortunately this meant that much of the work had to be done in the evenings, sometimes building hay ricks with Jan by moonlight. Beautiful certainly with a crescent moon shimmering in the black water of the loch at the foot of the fields, the hills of Jura purple in the distance and the hush of the Atlantic swell on the shore.

In 1968 a fierce storm with winds of more than 120 mph swept in from the west, blowing in the back door, lifting the kitchen linoleum with all the furniture, shifting it all to one corner and blowing out the window. The cow was calving in the byre and, having to go out to check, I had to crawl across the yard. Fortunately the byre roof had been replaced but the old corrugated iron sheets, which had been weighted down with boulders, flew around in the air like playing cards and some, like guillotine blades, sliced deep into the earth. Certain death for anyone in their path. Although the house rocked in the gale, the children slept through it all, including the new baby, our youngest (and last!).

Behind the house there was an ancient dry-stone sheep fank, In the spaces in the wall one could discover all kinds of fascinating objects – rusty shear blades, decaying sheep's horn, tins of archangel tar, empty bottles of lamb dysentery vaccine – an irresistible treasure trove for an inquisitive child. Our son, Jamie, found a bottle of liquid which looked like Coca-Cola, plucked out the cork and drank some of it. Within a few minutes he was almost unconscious. It was very old sheep dip, possibly containing arsenic. I lifted him into the Land Rover and rushed to the surgery, only to find that the doctor was out on his rounds. Driving with one hand and trying to keep Jamie awake with the other, I sped round the neighbourhood trying to locate the doctor. Eventually I found him and we returned to the surgery. The doctor spent precious time trying to get in touch with someone in a poisons department in Glasgow, as he did not believe a child could be foolish enough to drink dip. I was convinced that we should pump out the child's stomach immediately and we started to argue forcibly. Fortunately the District Nurse arrived and agreed with me, so she set up the equipment and siphoned out the poison. The smell of dip was unmistakeable. The nurse saved Jamie's life.

That year brought tragedy. My sister Mary, who had taken the stage name of Kate Story, was rehearsing with Diane Cilento in the Royal Court for *Maria* by Isaac Babel when she collapsed. Diane took her to her doctor who discovered that untreated cervical cancer had spread through her system. She died on 12 February at the Royal Marsden aged only 25 and leaving four children. A talented actress, she had appeared in five episodes of *Z Cars*, in *Out of the Unknown* (1965) and *Sergeant Cork* (1964). Her death affected me more than any other, perhaps because our parents chose not to tell me of her dying, so that I was unable to see her at the end.

Grief, like pain, is not a sensation that we learn. It erupts spontaneously from deep inside us, from a primeval core, tearing through tissues, howling in its urge to be born. Inexplicable, unpredictable, it claws its way out of our entrails, ravenous for words. Never. Nevermore. Quoth the raven. Unleashed by the finality of the loss, it leaps at us suddenly from darkness and daylight, from music and scents, from colours and touch. From the first cataclysm of its birth, it lurks in the shadows, waiting for a moment to spring. It never leaves. It does not diminish in ferocity. The most trivial things can trigger an attack – a piece of music, a shower of rain, a teaspoon in a cup, an involuntary oath. Time does not heal, it obscures.

I wrote a poem to her at the time:

Softly, sister,
Sail softly into the mist –
I would sooner not hear the wind in your ropes
Nor your ship's bow wave
Whispering through the sea.
I can see the empty hold and barren deck –
If I had known, I would have covered them with flowers
And bound the sun at the masthead.
If I had known, I would have pierced the dark
With heart-tallow candles or the brightness of my tears
But you must sail alone.
Better this than the last child you bore,
Ravenous and indestructible,
That let your life away in the deluge of its birth.
I know nothing now
Only that the mists close behind your ship
But I will light a candle
In the deepest temple of the earth
In case there is a heaven
And you lose your way.

Mary's premature death led to irreparable splits within the family over decisions about the children. The oldest two were placed with Ronnie Wilkinson's family without any argument. The twins were a different matter. We were keen to see them adopted but they were placed with my mother in Ireland, who by that time had founded her rather dubious religious community providing shelter and 'divine' therapy for the fragile children of wealthy gentry. Not the ideal environment for vulnerable young children, as it attracted such a variety of exceptionally odd creatures.

When our last was born, Jan stayed with my mother in Ireland as we could not get help on the farm. Sally claims to be the only truly Irish member of the family, apart from myself. By this time my mother's 'religious' community was firmly established and we were glad to leave before the children were infected, returning to Mull as quickly as we could.

Our children were all brought up to help on the farm – feeding dogs, cats or lambs, helping with the hay, lifting potatoes, gathering sheep or cattle or packing wool. In those days the sheared wool was packed in huge bags which were hung from a tall frame or in the rafters, and to pack the wool firmly someone had to climb into the bag and tread it tight. The girls found this to be great fun and emerged black with grease. They all had chores and were taught that the beasts were every bit as important as themselves. Their lives were not all hard work, though, for there was always music and stories. *The Hobbit* was one of the favourites. I read them most of Tolkien at bed time and sang the little ones to sleep with Irish lullabies and Scottish folksongs. On car journeys they relished songs with swear-words or risqué allusions, or revolutionary ballads like the 'Foggy Dew' or 'Bandiera Rosa'.

Finally we decided, with great reluctance, that we would have to leave Saorphin. Financially we were running very fast to keep still. We had applied to the Highland Fund, a precursor of the HIDB but infinitely better attuned to the needs of crofters, for help to buy some cattle, but we could wait no longer for a decision. Sadly, the offer came through as we left. In some ways it was a great relief to return to herding for someone else, and it was certainly a pleasure to have electricity and a washing machine – no more searching in the dark for the Tilley lamp primer in its jar of methylated spirits and the elusive box of matches. And so we moved. This time to herd Ben Lomond and live near Rowardennan.

We were near 'civilisation' again! We could have an evening out in Glasgow and people could visit us. We were able to see Ronnie Wilkinson who was playing Falstaff in the Citizens Theatre and Johnnie Rees who was appearing in the Close Theatre Club. Johnnie, one of Harold Pinter's closest friends, had lived in the flat above my sister in Chiswick and was a splendid character actor and a kind and generous person. Perhaps too generous, as he agreed to act as co-respondent in Pinter's divorce. Ronnie by this time had a serious alcohol problem and, on the last night, displayed it on stage.

In August 1969 we managed to escape for a holiday, taking all five children and the canoe to Scoraig. The settlement had changed considerably since my exploratory visit five years previously. Tom Forsyth had a habitable croft house and other families had arrived. There were tensions, however, which the immigrants had brought with them. The two ex-servicemen, who had created the most prolific fruit and vegetable garden on the barren peninsula, claimed that Tom was persecuting them. Quite elderly and fragile, they seemed to be truly fearful of him. We were shocked but could not check the veracity of their complaints. We had dinner with them, having caught a massive lithe while fishing from the canoe, and were shown round the magnificent garden while trying to soothe their apprehension.

Tom, at times, could act impulsively, some might say irrationally. Having formed a deep bond with the salmon fisherman's wife, he celebrated the intensity of the relationship by setting fire to the empty church. He was charged with arson and one of the final conditions of his case was that he would attend a clinic for psychiatric help. He assured me that this was completely unnecessary and that he knew more about the complexities of the human mind than the doctor – a claim which might well have been true.

Herding Ben Lomond was not the easiest of tasks. At lambing time hill walkers, with the best of intentions, would lift what they thought was an abandoned lamb and take it down to the hotel to be cossetted. I had to leave the farm, fetch the lamb from the hotel, carry it out to the hill and return it to its mother which by then was searching frantically for her offspring. It paid me to know by sight every ewe and new-born lamb on the Ben. In those days shepherds took a pride in knowing their flocks, a knowledge which is not too difficult to acquire of Blackface sheep but astonishing in shepherds of Cheviot or white face ewes.

The bond between a shepherd and his or her flock was unshakeable. It was that bond that ended my time on Ben Lomond.

The flockmaster, in his determination to force some of my gimmers to eat concentrates, shut them in a pen with the pellets, thinking that starvation would bend them to his will. Blackfaces are not so easily persuaded and they went on hunger strike. After a few days watching them get thinner I became furious.

'If one of those beasts dies,' I said, 'I'm leaving.'

'Well, you can just go now then.'

And so we moved.

Back to Argyll to Kilberry, an estate owned by the family of Coats of Paisley, the thread manufacturers. It was like stepping back in time. Workers were called by their surnames – even the Coats children displayed this habit of superiority to the staff. On arrival the estate owner addressed me as 'Orr'.

'My name,' says I, 'is Mr Orr or Willie.'

Completely aghast, he chose the latter. I don't think he meant to offend. It was merely expressive of his attitude towards the lower orders. The estate was run like that. Staff were not allowed to leave the place without permission and the owners felt free to walk into the houses at any time. Feudal, really.

It was at Kilberry that I damaged my back shearing and had to have a laminectomy. While in lying in hospital in Glasgow I received notice terminating my employment. A worker with a health risk was of no use to Coats. Being in a tied cottage, this meant the threat of eviction for our family. In spite of incapacity and the prospect of a long recovery, I was offered another position elsewhere. News of this treatment spread among the herds and it took him two years to find a replacement. Feudal indeed.

The new herding was at Auchreoch in Tyndrum with the best employer in our long list. Martin Cruickshank was a retired major from the Gordon Highlanders and had served in Malaya. He had a fascination for the Sahara and had crossed it north to south on a motorcycle and returned to it as often as he could. I was left in charge of the sheep, a responsibility which suited me admirably, my immune system being dangerously intolerant of 'bosses'. I herded Beinn Dubhchraig across from Ben Laoidh. It was a fair distance from the house and, in the summer, I had to leave at 3.30 am to be out at the march for the gathering. The dawn was often spectacular with the heather covered in a glistening gossamer mantle and the mist still swirling along Loch Lomond. There were seven herds in the area then and we helped each other to gather the sheep and work with them in the fanks, That neighbouring system built a strong community, which sadly came to an end as one after another the grazings were taken over for forestry.

By coincidence our nearest neighbour, Donald MacLean, had herded Ben Lomond immediately before me with his companion, Donald MacDiarmid – the 'two Donalds' as they were known. Old MacDiarmid had been a herd since he was a boy and, as a youth, had driven ewe hoggs by road from the west to the east coast by road for wintering, remaining there with the flock till the spring. Always recognisable from a distance, he wore a battered trilby hat and jacket which had seen many lambings in the hills. He lived alone with his dog Sweep. From him I received the greatest compliment of my life. When his hirsel was sold off for forestry, we stood together after the last gathering, watching the last lorry leaving, and he turned to me with his eyes brimming and said, 'So that's it then, eh? All gone. Don't suppose there'll be sheep here ever again. Don't suppose there'll be shepherds either. They don't make shepherds like us any more.'

Donald MacLean, originally from Harris, had a dog called Davey. Davey didn't need, or listen to, commands. He knew instinctively what to do. At a gathering in the high hills he would appear near you on the ridge and glance across as if to make sure you were behaving and then disappear. I had a pup off Davey called Smoke, pure grey and every bit as wise as her father. Donald's wife, Kathy, became a second mother to our girls as they spent so many hours in her kitchen helping with the baking. She came from a remarkable family in Harris in which four of the brothers became sea captains. Kathy and Donald are dead now, but they will always be remembered in our family with amusement and affection.

Our other neighbour was John Burton at Cononish whose farm included Ben Laoidh. He was the first to bring Swaledale sheep into the area, insisting that the ewes were better mothers than Blackfaces and that they reared more lambs. Being a Blackface enthusiast I teased him that Swales were really a kind of goat. We competed for the top price for lambs at Dalmally sales. Reluctantly I had to admit that Swales were more profitable.

Cononish is now renowned for its gold mine, the only commercial gold mine in Scotland. The long seam of quartz, which stretches from Meall Odhar on the Glencoe road south through Beinn Chuirn to the foot of Beinn Laoigh, has been mined for lead since 1739 and the old tailings from these can still be seen on the hillsides. Our children spent many hours hunting through the spoil and the old shafts for quartz crystals, lead ore and traces of gold. Sometimes one of them would hurry across with a piece of quartz glittering with traces of precious metal, only to be told that it was iron pyrites or 'fool's gold'. All that glitters . . .

In Tyndrum we met a couple from Czechoslovakia who were to become lifelong friends. The strange thing was we only met once on a wet afternoon and never met again. Ivan Krysl could speak no English and I had no Czech but we formed a bond which lasted till he died. In 1968, when Dubcek's attempt at democratic socialism was crushed by Soviet tanks, I had listened to Radio Free Prague late into the night and heard its last broadcast. 'Will you remember us when Czechoslovakia is no longer news?' it said. In protest a student called Jan Palach burnt himself to death in Wenceslas Square and I had written a poem for him. Ivan took it back to Prague. The couple had only been allowed to visit Scotland in 1973 because Ivan's wife, Ivana, was a plastic surgeon and had operated successfully on a leading Communist official. Their return to Prague was ensured by them having to leave children behind. They did go back and became members of Charter 77, a dissident group with Vaclav Havel campaigning for democracy. Their years of dangerous activity were rewarded in 1989. We kept in touch through the years, Ivana being able to speak English, and their children are now close friends of our children. Both Ivan and Ivana are dead now and their leaving has left an extraordinary gap in our lives.

PB visited us in Tyndrum on that memorable occasion when he introduced 'Mrs Stone'. He was on his best behaviour – charming, amusing, engaging. His warmth towards his grandchildren contrasted with his stern approach to his children when we were young. He entertained them with stories and a genuine interest in what they had to say. I watched him and thought of the wasted years when, had he showed us the same affection, we might have had a more honest and easier relationship.

We visited him in London in 1972 where he was living in a magnificent houseboat on Tagg's Island in the Thames. Like a

Mississippi river boat, it had two storeys, a balcony at either end, a reception room on the top deck stretching the entire length of the craft and all modern conveniences. It was a wonderful setting. You could lie in bed watching the ripples of the water on the ceiling and listening to the coots in the reeds. The gentle rocking as a cruiser passed lulled you into a contented trance. He and Marion had found an idyllic refuge from Westminster. But it was not to last.

1973 saw the last of my herding days. An event occurred which changed my life and that of the family.

13

Captain Orr was going to get married. Enoch Powell wrote on 7 August 1974 to wish him well.

> Dear Willy,
> Jim tells me that you are being married next week. This brings my warmest good wishes for your future happiness – indeed the future happiness of you both. You have fought an uphill fight and, if I may say so, with great courage. I hope you will be rewarded. Needless to add, Pam joins me in all this.

This while he was fishing for the South Down selection.

The lady concerned was Julia, the elegant lady in the camel-hair suit. He had bought an engagement ring costing more than £2,000. There were three problems though. The first that he was not divorced, his marriage being finally dissolved in April 1976. The second that he did not have £2,000. The third was that the bride was a Catholic and he was Imperial Grand Master of the Orange Order. The guests, including eminent Tory politicians like John Gorst were all assembled in Caxton Hall, Westminster and the bride was waiting, her anxiety increasing as the groom's time of arrival passed. That was when she phoned, the conversation recorded in the first pages of this memoir.

He did not appear and the bride had to cancel the ceremony. In the ensuing pandemonium he could not be found anywhere.

Shortly afterwards I received a phone call from Special Branch enquiring about his whereabouts. Still in the Highlands of Scotland, I had no idea. The officer explained that I was legally the next of kin and that he could not declare PB a missing person without my agreement.

'He is not missing,' I insisted. 'He has, quite sensibly, fled from the scene. He has "done a bunk" as we say in the family and will have gone somewhere to get his head together.' Special Branch, being used to covering for Members' indiscretions, naturally understood. Julia, however, being desperately upset and worried, urged me to declare him missing. As the days passed she lost patience with my casual approach and shrieked down the phone in frustration.

'Do you not care? He might be lying in a ditch. He might be in the hands of the IRA.'

Though these were possibilities, I was sure that he was safe and in hiding.

Then we had a call from his political agent in Ulster asking if I knew where he was and explaining that, as the constituency re-selection meeting was imminent, he needed to know if PB was intending to stand again He also mentioned that, lurking in the shadows with an interest in the seat, was the sinister figure of Enoch Powell. I was tempted to cause havoc in the enemy camp but refrained, and politely told the agent that I would pass on the message. Jim Molyneux also phoned and I replied in a similar manner.

Eventually I capitulated and booked a call through to Special Branch for 10 pm on the night before the re-selection meeting. However, BBC had got wind of the incident and on the evening news showed his photograph and reported that the MP for South Down was thought to be missing. A few minutes later he phoned me to say he was safe. We were relieved but also concerned for his future.

Naturally the affair with Julia ended abruptly and the woman with whom he had been living was also devastated and could not bear to have him back.

He did not stand again and relinquished his seat. Sinking into obscurity, he took a position as a receptionist in a London hotel. He had lost everything and was in debt. Jan travelled down to London to see him and tried to persuade him to talk to his sons. He confessed that he was too ashamed to see us.

A man, whose irresistible charm and handsome appearance attracted women too successfully, became, at that point, a rather sad, lonely recluse, burdened with guilt. Yet that was not the end of the story.

In the meantime life had changed for us. The previous year I had been involved in a tractor accident on the main road in which a lorry ran over my leg. When I was taken by ambulance to Stirling Infirmary, the surgeon was about to amputate below the knee when he noticed on the file that I was a shepherd and decided to save the leg. He operated and bound all the bits of bone together on a plate. Thanks to his skill, I still have the leg. The steel plate is still there and sets off security alarms at airports and channel ports.

One remarkable aspect of the accident was the response of our neighbours in Tyndrum. By the time Jan returned from hospital that night she found two lists – one of people to drive her down to visit me in hospital, the other of neighbours to look after the children while she was away. The local farming community, built round the neighbouring system, rallied to help us. That's how it was then, but as four large hirsels disappeared under sitka spruce, the system was weakened as shepherds and their families were forced to leave.

I was a very poor patient and not easy to live with. The children had to take over all my farming chores and many of the jobs round the house. The years of taking responsibility paid off and they were an invaluable support to both Jan and their irascible father.

While I was recovering our employer decided to sell off my part of the hill grazings to Economic Forestry, which was then paying exorbitant prices for land. So, with my leg in a stookie, the future looked pretty grim. The Forestry offered work for a year to organise the selling of the sheep stock and I did try to return to the hills, but found the pain in the leg unbearable. I could have taken a low-ground herding but that did not have the same manly status as the high hills, so I plunged into the unknown and applied for University.

While I was off work my white dog had developed a heart condition and had to be put down. I remember leaning on my crutches, barely able to watch her being driven away to the vet's, and turning away, feeling that I had lost part of myself. At the last gathering of the sheep on my hirsel Roy disappeared. No-one saw him leave and no-one could find him. A few days later a railway worker came to the house with a hind leg which was undoubtedly his. He had been killed on the railway. Shortly afterwards I gave Smoke on loan to a shepherd in Arrochar on the condition that, should I fail at University, she would be returned. Sadly, he fell out with some men in the pub and, in revenge, they threw poisoned meat to his dogs. Davey's daughter, so wise and handsome, was no more and my working dogs were gone.

To apply for University may seem an extraordinary change of direction, but I had been interested in the politics of land use and had stood for the new local council as an SNP candidate. PB and his family naturally detested nationalism, equating the SNP with IRA. Through the SNP I met David Simpson, an economist who taught at Stirling University and so applied for a place there. I had no qualifications, but Stirling had an enlightened policy of allocating a number of places to 'mature' students, a risk which usually bore fruit, and so I enrolled in 1974 at the age of 34.

What an experience! I discovered History. At private school our history had been concealed from us. We learnt about Clive in India and Woolf in Quebec and the great British Empire but nothing about Ireland or the British working class. Having made the discovery, I launched into history with relish – not the history of kings and queens and 'great men' but the history of people. The pages of Hobsbawm, E.P. Thompson, A.J.P. Taylor and Engels opened out a whole new world. A Marxist analysis of industrialisation suddenly made sense, recognising the dynamic drive of capitalism and its inherent need to alienate and exploit working people. I consumed the stories of industrialisation in Japan, Britain and America and the economics of Imperialism with lecturers like Robin Law and Roy Campbell.

I had intended to study Economics and indeed completed a couple of years of the subject with a superb teacher called Mark

Brownrigg. I was particularly interested in regional economics but the subject disappeared from Stirling's curriculum, largely due to the procrastination of the University Court. At the time the Fraser of Allander Trust was considering establishing an Institute for research into the Scottish economy. The Court was approached but, in its usual fashion at that time, swithered. In the meantime, Strathclyde University, quick off the mark, secured the Institute, so Stirling not only lost the Institute but its team of excellent regional economists who transferred their skills to its rival. History, therefore, became my subject.

Inevitably I was drawn into student politics and joined the Communist Party with John Reid who was to become a Cabinet Minister and a Peer of the Realm. It was obvious to us all that John had ambitions far beyond the student scene and that the discipline of the Party would be a temporary yoke. Yet it was in the Party that he learnt about politics and the skills to deal with the far left. At that time the International Marxist group had taken a decision to penetrate the Labour Party and John learnt how to handle their tactics. I was told that John had a part in Neil Kinnock's speech for conference at Bournemouth in 1983 when Neil confronted the far left and, if that is the case, it was in Stirling that he developed the technique. It is said that if you are not a communist when you are young, you have no heart and, if you are still a communist when you are mature, you have no head. John outgrew the Party and moved into Labour politics, adopting its approach of pragmatism over principles. Many on the left saw this as a betrayal. On a personal level I still carry an affection and respect for him and for his first wife Kathy. I used to babysit for them while John was still a student – actually he seemed to be continually a student with a flair for negotiating extensions on his PhD year after year.

Like John, I became President of the Student Union and sat on the University Court, an enlightening but frustrating experience, and, like him, left the Party but never abandoned the principles of Socialism. During my time we founded the Anti-Apartheid Association and the Chile Defence Committee to support the refugees arriving in Scotland from Pinochet's brutal tyranny. Many of these young people had been imprisoned and tortured and were deeply traumatised. By good fortune there was a priest in Stirling who was fluent in Spanish and joined the Committee.

I have been asked what drew me to Socialism. Some have suggested that it was a form of rebellion against my father but, in all honesty, I don't think it was that. I have an intense aversion to injustice and a suspicion of authority, both of which I think stem from experiences in prep school and in the shipyard. Yet these lay dormant all through my late teenage years, resurfacing with my sister's death and the brutal response of the Protestant B Specials to the Civil Rights marches in Ulster. The feelings were stirred again by my accident and the sale of the hill I herded. At Stirling I found Marxist analysis a means of understanding the system in which injustice flourished and, in Socialism, an alternative to it.

Mind you, it is difficult to escape the injustice of being raised as the son of a Tory M.P., particularly if you embrace radical politics. It is easier to conceal the relationship, a habit which, however reasonable, leaves a sense of betrayal and guilt. Throughout my working life I have avoided talking about PB, largely because I found his association with the Orange Order distasteful and his praise for the B Specials unforgivable. When the link with him is discovered, it is immediately assumed that I have the same views and that I have been showered with privileges.

On 18 January 1976 I attended the inaugural meeting of a completely new political party in the Grosvenor Hotel in Glasgow. The atmosphere was vibrant with enthusiasm, hope and determination. Journalists like Neal Ascherson and Ruth Wishart were there to record the excitement. The ill-fated Scottish Labour Party was born that afternoon. The leading figure was Jim Sillars who, in a most eloquent and inspiring speech, declared, 'We are Scottish with a capital S and Socialist with a capital S.' I became a founder member of the Party and still have my party card!

The Labour Party in Scotland at that time was stubbornly ambivalent about devolution and the Scottish Council at one point had opposed the notion. Yet many in the party, wise enough to recognise the threat of the SNP, were disenchanted with the leadership and, outside the party, could see that there was a growing appetite for a new socialist vision. The crucial issue was control over the Scottish Development Agency and, when it became clear that the national Labour Party was failing to grant this, the frustrated 'mini-cadre' of Sillars and Alex Neil and others launched the new party.

It was to be a democratic party with no trade union block votes, and power theoretically vested in the branches. It was to be allied to the Socialist International and to Europe. 'Scotland in Europe' was a central policy. Jim Sillars, having campaigned vigorously with the SNP against membership of the EEC, suddenly became a convert, recognising the result of the referendum – 58% of Scottish voters for the EEC and 42% against.

At the first national conference held later that year I was expelled from the party – along with some others – for disruptive behaviour at Conference. This was bizarre as I was not at the meeting! I did receive an apology from Alex Neil but, like many others, was sufficiently disenchanted to reject 'rejoining'. Hamish Henderson described the affair as a 'witch-hunt'. The National Organising Committee, in its rush to expel ultra-left members such as International Marxists and Socialist Workers, lashed out at anyone resembling a subversive. Having not devised a plan to deal with penetration by the hard left, the leaders allowed the party to tear itself apart. Its slow, painful death was sad to watch.

The coterie of mature students to which I was drawn was probably typical of such student groups in the 70s with a wide variety of backgrounds and trades. We had a house painter, a bricklayer, a bookie's runner, a shipyard worker and a hill shepherd, all of whom graduated. Unlike students today, our return to education was encouraged by a generous grant system. I had the advantage of a maintenance grant, a two homes allowance, a mature student's allowance and an allowance for our five children. I imagine that, like all the others, I have repaid that in tax. Our small group formed the kernel of what was called the Broad Left, a concept based on Gramsci's philosophy, and provided most of the student leaders. Our sworn enemies were the 'Trots', the Socialist Workers and the International Marxist Group.

Knowing of the IMG's plan to infiltrate the Labour Party we warned the latter of the policy. The Party refused to listen and suffered painfully from the abscess in its flesh.

Devolution, of course, was a major issue in the 1970s with Gordon Brown's *The Red Paper on Scotland* helping to promote the debate. In 1975 the Rectors and Honorary Presidents of the Scottish Universities met as a group to discuss the implications for institutions. However, from a meeting in January 1976 a press statement was issued indicating support for devolution. This alarmed some of the Rectors, particularly Magnus Magnusson of Edinburgh who distanced himself from the group and political involvement, concerned that it 'was increasingly being used as a forum for political expression and action'. Heaven forbid that Rectors should be accused of political activism. Magnusson and the four other Rectors (Iain Cuthbertson, Clement Freud, Alan Coren and Arthur Montford) withdrew from the group, leaving only Alex Main, Tony Martin and myself to carry the torch.

Tony accused the Rectors of elitism. 'The Rectors are now holding private meetings and I find this disgraceful. This is as elitist as the behaviour of the university principals. The universities need open government, not a return to the Middle Ages . . . They were elected to represent student policies.'

The *Scotsman* carried the headline, 'Rectors shun call to devolve universities' which was a slight distortion of the situation but pleased us enormously. I rarely watched *Mastermind* without recalling Magnusson's sniffy dismissal of the 'red-brick' Presidents. I have never felt the same about *Mastermind* since then.

I have fond memories of Stirling and my small group of friends gathered in the kitchen of the residence in the evening while sharing herbal tobacco and listening to the Eagles. It was not all humourless politics and heated discussion. We had time to go to discos, to gather wild mushrooms, to cook Hungarian goulash and even write the odd essay. A second childhood really. Sadly, five of the old comrades have passed away and we are left wondering who is next to go.

While I was in Stirling I met Tom Buchan again who was giving poetry readings to the students. By this time he was editor of the radical magazine *Scottish International* and was an acclaimed poet and playwright. His *Dolphins at Cochin* had been published in 1969 and his hilarious satirical play *Tell Charlie Thanks for the Truss* had been staged at the Traverse. As Tom McGrath said, the format of Tom's play with song, dance and humour was the forerunner of *The Cheviot, the Stag and the Black, Black Oil*. Tom was in great spirits, at the peak of his career and happier than ever, but that was two years before he parted from Alice. I still have the small book of poems he gave me that night.

I am left with one great regret. During those four years at Stirling I left Jan and the children in Tyndrum. She was left to cope with five children on her own. Although I came home at weekends and holidays, they maintain that I came back in body but not in mind. I've no doubt this is true and that the boys particularly suffered from the absence. Yet it did have some positive effects, for Jan became more of an independent woman and my years in University eventually led to a professional salary.

14

My first employment after graduating in 1978 was with the HIDB. Ironically this was the organisation which I had attacked so vehemently in 1966. On this occasion I was offered a short contract to assess one of its projects. Immediately after the UK joined the EEC in 1973 a group of 64 astute farmers in North Argyll, seizing an opportunity to squeeze extra funding from Europe, formed an association to submit an application. Assisted by the HIDB the farmers devised an ambitious scheme costing £1.4 million over five years which they hoped would attract a grant of £370,000 from Europe. The money was to be used to improve the land and thereby increase the numbers of sheep and cattle. Unfortunately the scheme was launched just as there was a catastrophic collapse in store cattle prices and an equally destructive increase in costs, so many of the plans had to be abandoned. My task was to ascertain exactly how many projects were shelved and therefore how much less European money would be needed. The farmers were pleased to speak to someone with experience and opened their accounts willingly. I found that 30% of the schemes would not be completed and that £170,000 of the EEC money could be re-allocated, so my meagre wage over five months had released a six-figure sum in Europe.

It was a fascinating piece of work, taking me to islands like Lismore, Kerrera and Seil and to remote farms in Morvern, Mull and Lorn. I met progressive farmers like the Cadzows who had developed the Luing cattle breed, aristocrats like Sir Charles MacGrigor whose wife became a distinguished author, hard-working stocksmen like Willie Dickie of Musdale and business-men like Peter Shand-Kydd, the stepfather of Princess Diana, who farmed at Ardencaple on the Isle of Seil.

In spite of this short sojourn in proper work, I prolonged my self-indulgence in academia by starting on a PhD, having obtained an Honours degree. I had heard Tom Devine lecturing in the staff club at Stirling and was determined to work under him in Strathclyde. I reckoned that, if someone could talk for an hour and a half on Highland history without mentioning sheep, he must be either rather dim or of exceptional intellect. Tom, I think, came into the latter category. My year with him, research-ing the development of deer forests in the Highlands, was so stimulating that I was reluctant to abandon the work. Yet it was leading me into greater debt, so I was forced to bring it to an end. Besides, I had been away from the family for far too long as it was, so I applied for teacher training at Jordanhill. I can safely say that that year was the greatest waste of time in my career, many of the tutors having lost touch with classrooms, and, had it not been for the time I spent completing the Strathclyde thesis, I might have left the College. The thesis was published and gained me a Masters degree, so the effort was not in vain.

And so I became a teacher of History and Modern Studies in Oban High School in Argyll – quite a change from both shep-herding and living a second childhood at Stirling. As it happened, all our children were students in Oban and all but the eldest, who resisted the opportunity to be embarrassed, appeared in my classes at some point. I cannot claim to have taught them – that would be a distortion of the truth – but I droned on in front of each of them about the early iron industry or radical trade unions. My second son, Jamie, developed the technique of appearing to listen intently while his mind was elsewhere. One daughter fell asleep in the class.

In those days the male and female staff staggered into different staffrooms at break and lunch times. In the male one, which was little larger than a broom cupboard, there were five pipe-smokers, so we emerged from its toxic depths bleary-eyed and smelling like kippers. The female room, known as the 'snake pit', was just across from ours but we never entered it except in desperation. If we ran out of sugar, we drew lots for the mission to cross the corridor as the human sacrifice.

The belt or the tawse was still the preferred instrument of pupil control, a form of punishment I never used, preferring intimidation or emotional abuse. That's not strictly true. I tried to engage with the youngsters, showing them some respect and treating them as adults, hoping to receive some respect in return. The tawse was a leather strap 20-24 inches long, split into three tails at one end to inflict the maximum pain. There was a firm in Lochgelly in Fife which produced these barbaric implements for Scottish teachers. In my second year the local authority decided to abolish the belt. The policy was introduced without any real consideration of the result nor the development of a proper alternative. Some older staff were left floundering and seriously stressed. Unlike them, I had been out in the wide world working for a living and that experience gave me confidence in the classroom. Also I liked children, a characteristic which I found to be lacking in the majority of secondary teachers.

In those days Scottish teachers were a militant lot, their union, the EIS, being one of the stronger members of the STUC. In Oban we formed the first Trades Council, bringing together delegates from many of the trades and professions in the district, and organised the first union march in support of NHS nurses' pay. The head teacher opposed the formation of the Trades Council, so we conspired successfully to remove him from the National Council of the EIS. Militant indeed.

As part of the Modern Studies course we took a group of students to the Soviet Union in 1983, a time when it was still a relatively closed country. When I woke in Leningrad on the first morning and looked out at the cranes of an immense building programme, I felt reassured that, in spite of the political deficiencies and brutal abuses of human rights, there was a side of the Socialist state which was working. I had carried with me a letter of fraternal greetings from the Trades Council for the Soviet equivalent of the TUC and arranged a meeting with Russian officials in Moscow, travelling to the offices by Metro. After the meeting they insisted on providing me with a car to take me back to the hotel. So there I was, gliding sedately through the streets of the city in a long black chauffeur-driven limousine in perfect comfort.

'Yes,' I thought, 'This is the rock on which revolutions founder.'

Perhaps this sensation of well-being and status was what PB found irresistible in the UK.

While in Leningrad, we visited the Hermitage, a truly amazing experience. I felt that I could easily spend a week in its vast precincts, absorbing the art, the sculpture and the museum pieces. Founded on a collection purchased from southern Europe by the lascivious Catherine the Great in 1764, it is a magnificent display of human creativity. There are at least a dozen Rembrandts, Michelangelo's 'Crouching Boy' and paintings by Raphael, Caravaggio, Picasso, Gainsborough and Reynolds. It is the largest single collection of paintings in the world and has a range and depth which is astonishing. While I walked through the Palace I remembered that my father had been there in 1953 and had been equally impressed.

Jan and I had our first foreign holiday shortly after the Russian trip, flying to Yugoslavia. It was still a unified Socialist country with images of Tito displayed in the streets. Its form of 'market socialism' claimed to be a compromise between free-market capitalism and rigid state control. Tito had defied the Soviet Union in establishing an independent system and was highly regarded in the West as a 'benevolent dictator'. Makarska, the village in which we stayed, had been his headquarters during the war and the buildings still bore the marks of the ferocious battles fought in its streets. A visit to the graveyard showed how the village suffered from Nazi reprisals and lost so many of its young men as partisans.

Initially we were treated with unusual reserve, a coldness verging on hostility, until we discovered that we were thought to be German. Jan's long fair hair and blue eyes were the cause of the problem. When we were found to be Scots and that we knew Fitzroy MacLean, the attitude changed to enthusiastic welcome. During the war Winston Churchill had sent Fitzroy to Yugoslavia to decide which resistance group to support and he had recommended Tito's partisans. Fitzroy was a national hero and had a house on Korcula. It was a novel experience to stay in a hotel owned by the staff who expressed a genuine interest in our enjoyment of the visit. It was sad to read years later of the suffering of the Croatian people in the four years of the war between 1991 and 1995. We kept in touch with friends we had met there and knew from them the effect of the indescribable atrocities committed by the military during the war. Had Germany recognised the Croatian Republic in October 1991, the worst might have been avoided.

The effects of the war actually reached Tyndrum, as two sons of Major Cruickshank, our previous employer, fought on opposite sides; one as a mercenary, the other as a regular. Fortunately for the Major, they survived.

At home Jan and I and the family embarked on what was seen as a distinctly risky enterprise. Strathclyde Region had started a project called the Community Parents Scheme, through which difficult, damaged and deprived adolescents, who had been placed in residential List D schools, were fostered with families. After rigorous assessment we were approved and became foster parents. This was to be Jan's 'employment', but the work relied on the support of the whole family. Our children learnt what real deprivation meant and about the irreparable damage inflicted by emotional, physical and sexual abuse.

Folk in the village said, 'Are you not worried that these kids will lead yours astray?'

We hoped that it wouldn't be the other way round.

A couple of days after the first boy arrived we agreed to let him and our younger son take a tent and camp down in the garden. I visited the tent later in the evening to find them both as high as kites on glue! A salutary lesson. The first boy, Steven, was a delightful rogue. We all adored him but the local high school could not cope with his behaviour and he had to leave us. I can still see his face in the rear window of the car as he left the house. Sadly his solvent abuse progressed into heroin after he left.

On the day that Princess Diana and Charles were married I had decided to be as far away as geographically possible from the whole affair and trekked to the remote heights of Ben Alder in the central Highlands. I took Steven and No. 2 son with me. We took the train to Corrour Station and set off through the rain towards the first ridge above Loch Ossian. It was a dismal day. Having erected the mountain tent near the top and cooked tea inside, I looked out to find that the sky had cleared to reveal a truly magnificent view over the hills. Steven was sulking in the back of the tent.

'Steven,' I said, 'come and see this.'

He crawled to the entrance.

'That's fucken magic!' he gasped.

We used to hear of Steven periodically during his spells in prison but, many years later, I heard his voice on the phone. Another young offender, who had moved with his mother to Glasgow, phoned and asked me to guess who was with him. I couldn't, naturally, but in the background I heard Steven say, 'Ask Willie if he remembers the tent.'

So, all through those years in and out of prison, he had remembered Ben Alder, perhaps one of the few good memories he had treasured.

Tom Buchan came to stay with us while we were in Dalmally and told us the sad story of his split with Alice. He said that he had arrived home to find his friend and her together *in flagrante delicto,* a scene which he could not expel from his memory and a shock from which he never really recovered. He was, nevertheless, as entertaining as ever. He showed us a draft of 'King Brude of the Picts', which sent our children into paroxysms of hilarity, and he kept them amused for hours with his bawdy stories. Yet we were to see the darker side of him when he moved to a caravan in North Connel and almost destroyed himself with a prolonged spell of drinking. A friend alerted us to his condition and we arrived to find him in a sorry state. We managed to dress him, help him into the car and drive him to rehabilitation in Glasgow. I never saw him again. He ended up in Forres and, in October 1995, was found dead in the woods near Findhorn.

Tom's son, Lawrence, who had been at school with our son, married Mairi Hedderwick's daughter from Coll and, after they separated, he used to stay with us when he came to collect his daughter, Sophie, for holidays. By extraordinary coincidence she became one of my 'clients' in Oban High School. The spectre of Tom Buchan, like Banquo's ghost, seemed to appear from the shadows now and then to remind me of his existence.

15

I left teaching for the first time in 1985 after the teachers' strikes that year. In the face of pay cuts the EIS demanded a pay review body which the Government naturally opposed. One of our colleagues, a Maths teacher called John J. Mackay, who had become a Tory M.P., still lived in Oban and had children at the school, so we were selected as one of the 'target' schools for strike action. One of the policies was to withdraw from extra-curricular activities such as team games and, as a result, many teachers 'got a life' and rediscovered fulfilling interests and hobbies. They did not renew their commitment to extra hours after the strike. The action won but it was a Pyrrhic victory, as stringent conditions of service were attached.

I had resolved to leave the profession anyway. I found myself becoming tetchy and impatient with the youngsters, so I reckoned it was time to go. Of all the jobs I had undertaken, teaching was the most stressful. I felt sorry for the staff as I left for a less demanding post.

I left to work as a researcher for Tom Devine on a study of the great famine that swept through Scotland in the 1840s after the failure of the potato crop. It was a fascinating piece of work, examining estate papers held in the Record Office and original census books completed by local enumerators. Tom published the results in *The Great Highland Famine*.

While searching in the papers of the Dukes of Argyll in Inveraray Castle, I came across many references to a township called Shiaba on the Ross of Mull. It is one of the many deserted villages on the island from which the Gaels had been evicted during the famine. The ruins stand above the cliffs facing the sea. Moss grows on the hearthstones where the peat fires burned and the lintels have cracked over the empty windows. The township is pervaded with an air of melancholy as if the exiles had left behind their sorrow. Yet some of the letters from the first people who left for Canada are full of promise and attempts to persuade others to follow. The Ross of Mull lost 40% of its people and never really recovered from the loss. I used to gather sheep through Shiaba, so the details I found in the records had a special meaning for me.

I persuaded Tom Devine to visit the area, and out of this arose his interest in the Ross and the foundation of the Ross of Mull Historical Society. An unusual aspect of the emigration from the parish during the famine is that the journey and destination of the islanders is described in the records, and one of the founders of the Society was able to visit their graves and descendants near Owen Sound in the Great Lakes.

Our children had all left school by this time and so we abandoned the fostering scheme, having had quite a number of youngsters through the household. However, without our children, there was no point in continuing as we relied heavily on them to help with the foster children. The scheme, nevertheless, had given us an insight into the Children's Panel system and social work practice and this experience was to prove invaluable later.

After the research contract ended I had a choice – return to teaching or work as a researcher with BBC Aberdeen. Jimmie

MacGregor was involved in filming one of his many walks across Scotland and asked me to work with his team. Very tempting, but it was temporary and the position might have been that of a mere 'gofer'. I returned to teaching in Selkirk, a small school with no behaviour problems, as everyone in the town knew each other and every student leaving the school found employment. We found an extraordinary place to stay.

The Haining was an ancient estate set in the middle of Selkirk but strangely isolated from the town, a rural enclave with its own lake and mansion dating back to the seventeenth century. The owner was something of a recluse, preferring the company of the scores of cats which were imprisoned within the decaying mansion. The building had been neglected and the rain dripped in through the cupola, coating many of the antiques in a mantle of mould. There was a remarkable collection of paintings but one had to step round the cat shit to examine them. When he died he left the estate to the people of Selkirk, a gesture of generosity which left them with a crippling challenge.

In Selkirk I met Paddy Ashdown again, having not seen him since our preparatory school in Bangor. I had invited David Steel in to the school to speak to the Modern Studies class about politics and had mentioned that Paddy had been a school friend. At the time David was relinquishing the leadership of the Liberal Party and Paddy was visiting him to discuss the matter. David invited me over to renew the contact. Paddy reminded me of my attempt to drown him when we were children, an incident which I had naturally erased from memory. I had built a raft out of old wood and oil drums and needed to test its seaworthiness, so I persuaded Paddy to sit on it while I pushed it out to sea. I did keep hold of the rope but his mother came storming down to the shore like a galleon in full sail and gave me a fearful row. Paddy, in his autobiography, gives a slightly different – and more generous – account of the incident. Still, I can claim that the Liberal Party owes a great deal to my nascent skills as a marine engineer.

Sadly, while I was writing this story, I learnt of Paddy's death, so those memories of our childhood together are particularly poignant and precious, emerging from a time of innocence and contentment. Once we laid our hands on his father's ceremonial swords and, with a cry of '*en garde*', we fenced balletically in the bedroom to the tune of Ravel's *Bolero*. Now, when I hear the melody, I remember him and his father's horror when we were caught. Paddy grew up to be a remarkable person, one of that very rare and vanishing species – a politician with integrity. He will be missed.

In Selkirk I taught Modern Studies, a subject which has always been regarded with suspicion by conservatives. As I was keen to attract adults into the school, the head teacher placed his wife in my Higher class. I'm sure she was there to report on any political bias or indoctrination on my part. However I arranged to take the class to Ravenscraig which was under attack by Margaret Thatcher's government and introduced her and the others to the chief shop steward. There she heard the tragic details of the impact on the Lanarkshire communities of the loss of the steelworks. We studied UK politics and women's issues, the benefit system and housing. The lady, I'm delighted to say, formed her own opinion, which was far from conservative, and went back to further education. At no point was I accused of bias. Enlightenment was enough.

While in Selkirk I was given a Writer's Bursary by the Scottish Arts Council and Borders Region granted me a sabbatical to write. Although I was working on an historical novel at the time, I misused the opportunity by finishing a travel book on Argyll. Had we been relying on *Discovering Argyll, Mull and Iona* for a living we would not have survived the winter. Yet some of my short stories were being published and a few feature articles, and these hints of success tempted us back to Argyll where we planned to run a guest house for disabled people and earn a few pounds by writing. And so we moved.

16

We had kept our house in Dalmally, handing it over to our eldest son and daughter-in-law to run as a bed and breakfast business, so we were able to move back and build on an extension specially designed for wheelchair users. Tom Devine offered me another research contract which I couldn't resist, on this occasion investigating the Lowland Clearances. Some of the work involved reading through eighteenth-century Court of Session papers in the National Library, searching for information on agricultural change. In the course of this, however, I came across several cases involving black slaves in Scotland. This was fascinating as very little had been written about Scottish slavery. One case, that of a Jamie Montgomery, was particularly interesting because he had lived in my wife's home town of Beith and the proceedings were recorded in great detail. I had to follow it up and, hoping to discover more about Jamie, went across to West Register House to consult the records there. Not only did I find more detail but I actually held his Bill of Sale in my hand. That was a moving experience and inspired a lasting interest in slavery.

Robert Shedden of Beith, who had a plantation in Virginia, had sent Jamie to Beith as an apprentice carpenter to enhance his value. Returning home himself, however, he decided to ship Jamie back to America. Jamie, hearing that Christians could not be held as slaves, had himself baptised. The minister who performed the ceremony was John Witherspoon who, some years later, emigrated to America and was the only man of the cloth to sign the Declaration of Independence. Outraged, Shedden hired thugs to kidnap his property and put him aboard a ship. Jamie escaped and fled to Edinburgh, only to be caught and imprisoned. A long court case followed but was never resolved as Jamie died in the Tolbooth. Shedden's family are buried in the same churchyard as Jan's grandfather.

I discovered several other cases relating to slaves in Scotland and published a long piece in the *Scotsman* in June 1990 which encouraged others to research the subject. I even wrote a novel based on Jamie which lingers in a drawer somewhere.

The work for Tom sadly lasted only a year so I had to find another source of income. I contacted Oban High School to see if I could work as a supply teacher for a couple of days per week. Instead of teaching I was offered the opportunity to set up and manage a special project for disaffected and difficult young people. I was delighted. The experience of fostering and the contact which that involved with Social Work and the Childrens Panel was invaluable.

The local Education Officer insisted that I should be trained for the post, so enrolled me in St Andrews College, Bearsden, for a special diploma. At first I tried living in the residences through the week, but the students were so riotous at night that I couldn't sleep so I was forced to travel daily from Dalmally. I had to admit that I had outgrown student life. Middle age (or maturity) had crept in. Part of the training was in Gartnavel Adolescent Unit, a secure placement for seriously disturbed young people, where I learnt a great deal about treatment of severe conditions and the value of interdisciplinary co-operation. It was an invaluable and enlightening experience.

The project in Oban was based on a visionary report from Strathclyde Region entitled 'Young People in Trouble', recommending ways of dealing with troublesome adolescents in school. I set out to work with a group of twelve boys who were almost out of control. I saw each of them individually once a week to talk through their difficulties which were inevitably related to their homes. It was essential therefore to work with the parents and with any other agencies already involved. These could include social workers, psychologists, police, doctors, the Sheriff and psychiatrists.

Of the original twelve rogues, eight ended up in prison after school, so I suppose the first year couldn't be regarded as a resounding success. Yet we did establish a good relationship with them and this proved to be invaluable when I came to deal with their children later on. Imprisonment was a disaster for some of the boys as they picked up the heroin habit there and all the necessary contacts to satisfy it. Heroin had become a problem in Oban and there were no services available in the town. The local police and medical practices were in denial at the time, so the toxin spread through the community.

After the first year the project focused on younger students and included more girls. It began to show some success as an increasing number of youngsters were saved from exclusion and placement in residential schools, saving the council a great deal of money. At every stage, like most worthwhile services, it had to fight for funding. The primitive attitude prevailed that youngsters who caused trouble deserved punishment rather than help and support. Yet help was what they needed. In a third of the hundreds of cases one or both parents was alcoholic, living chaotic lives. A third also were from single parent families – not that this necessarily led to difficulties, but teenage boys do find it harder to deal with single mothers. As the mother has to change from care to control, the boy experiences the loss of his nurturing parent.

There were many cases of abuse with all the destructive effects of that. Strangely, I encountered more sexual abuse of boys than girls, two men in the catchment area accounting for most of the boys. One man lived in very remote cottage far from other people and contacted the boys through CB radio, eventually luring them to his fireside. A tall, strong man, so once they were there, they could not resist. Although one of them described the horrors of his visit, the police needed the corroboration of another to bring charges. Nothing was done till a year later, one of his victims, who had been taken into care elsewhere, confirmed the abuse. When the police arrived at the cottage with a citation the man collapsed with a heart attack and died. In a sense, perhaps this was justice, but the group of boys felt that they were deprived of the opportunity to face their abuser in court.

In another case, the victims were chosen carefully by the perpetrator's wife. They were all boys from a special school and the couple considered that they might be seen as unreliable witnesses in court, if they were caught. This case came to light many years later after the couple had left the area. The damage inflicted on these children is often revealed in aggressive or even criminal behaviour, the root of which is concealed in shame and terror. What adults see is delinquent behaviour. What the children feel is betrayal and pain. It was difficult to deal with them in school as the origin of the aggression could not be revealed to staff.

During my time with the Project I attended many Children's Hearings and developed a deep respect for the system. It is probably the most enlightened and progressive juvenile justice system in the world. Three ordinary citizens, who have been well trained, interview the child and his parents in the presence of a professional Reporter and decide on the best way forward for the child. They listen carefully to the child's point of view and can ask to speak to the child alone before coming to a decision. The whole procedure is informal and the interest of the child is central to the discussion. Also there to advise is a social worker and usually a teacher. The three Panel members can decide to have the child placed in care or returned home under the supervision of a social worker or to proceed no further.

The system has often been attacked either as too lenient on the one hand or too oppressive on the other. The most intense assault was in 1991 over the Orkney affair, when nine children taken into care and removed from the island. There were rumours of Satanic abuse and bizarre rituals as well as sexual abuse. The case attracted a deluge of hysterical reporting by the media, most of the fury being aimed at the Orkney social workers and the Reporter to the Children's Panel. The Hearing system, according to the press, was clearly flawed. Yet, when the parents appealed to the Sheriff and he ruled that the children should be flown home, the fact that his decision was part of the system was ignored. The system, in that respect, was working. When the Reporter, in turn, appealed to the Court of Session, Lord Hope upheld the social work case and commented that

Sheriff Kelbie had caused 'incalculable damage' by not allowing the evidence to be heard.

The truth, therefore, may never be known. However, I happened to be visiting a List D school when one of the Orkney children disclosed to a member of staff details of abuse and, having met the child, I had no doubt about the veracity of his story. The whole affair, particularly the poisonous reporting in the tabloid press, left the reputation of Hearings in tatters. However, it did lead to intensive re-examination of practices by all of us involved in Child Protection and to the Children (Scotland) Act of 1995. I was given the task of explaining the complexities of this Act to staff. A well-balanced report by Tom Devine and Richard Holloway in 2004 on Children's Hearings entitled 'Where's Kilbrandon Now?' did much to restore confidence in this unique and invaluable system. It did recognise what, in my experience, was one of the main weaknesses of the system. The Panel members might place a youngster under social work supervision but social workers were so overstretched and under-resourced that meaningful work with the family was impossible.

The school project and involvement in Child Protection left me with an intense admiration for the young people and their resilience in coping with impossible circumstances. Their courage, their loyalty and their humour were exemplary. It was a privilege to know them and do what I could to help them take charge of their lives.

Unfortunately the far-seeing Head Teacher who had launched the scheme retired. He had steadfastly supported it – sometimes against his staff – his view being that, if we showed the troubled young people that we cared, then, when they became parents, they would support the school in dealing with their children. The Head Teacher who followed him was less sympathetic, regarding myself and the project as subversive and anarchic. She closed it and I was transferred to conventional learning support. Nevertheless, she decided to bring in a 'behaviour specialist' to advise her on a new system. Sandy Peterson, much to her irritation, not only appreciated but even admired the work of the project. He had many years of experience in the field and had run a school for troubled children in Edinburgh. We formed a team to establish a behaviour regime based on our values. The project, however, was never restored in its original form.

In the early 1990s I was asked to write a regular column in the *Weekend Scotsman*, calling it the 'Rural Voltaire' in opposition to Jack MacLean's 'Urban Voltaire' in the *Glasgow Herald*. I didn't see it in that light and knew that it could not rival his wit and perspicacity. However, it was fairly scurrilous and provided the *Scotsman* lawyers with a little extra work. It ended in 1994 when Andrew Jaspan descended on the paper's unsuspecting team, slicing through them and their reporting like a scythe through corn. Modernising it was called. He didn't like my work so the column was one of the casualties. Still, Jaspan's whirlwind lasted only nine months, but it caused irreparable damage to the morale of the staff.

Through contacts in the *Scotsman* I managed to negotiate a splendid arrangement with Hoseason's tours through which they would offer a free holiday on the French canals if I wrote a descriptive piece in the newspaper. On the first of these we were given a small cruiser on the Canal du Midi, sailing from Bezier to Carcassonne, one of the most relaxing excursions we experienced. We were not permitted to sail faster than four miles an hour so we glided through the French countryside at a leisurely pace, sometimes looking down on the fields, sometimes passing through shaded avenues of plane trees. We could tie up in a village at night or choose an isolated spot in the complete silence of the countryside. On another occasion we were provided with a massive luxury cruiser on the Lot when the river was in spate, an adventure which was far from relaxing. The fast-flowing water constantly tried to tug the boat sideways so the person on the helm had to fight with the current every step of the way. Still, we did manage to see the magnificent cave paintings in Pech-Merle. It is a moving experience to look down on the footprint of a child made thousands of years ago and gaze on the exquisite drawings of animals on the walls. The sense of a connection with those primitive people lingers long after one emerges into the daylight.

17

While I was working with the young people and their families in the project it became obvious that Oban needed a free counselling service. People in crisis in the town were having to wait up to six weeks for help from support services, so Jan and I set out to gather an interested group to raise funds for proper training. We managed to obtain a grant from Lloyds TSB and employed professional trainers to provide a COSCA Certificate in Counselling in 1997 for twelve volunteers, five of whom were men. This was the beginning of Lorn Counselling Service, which by 2001 was providing a free and immediate service to people suffering from anxiety, bereavement, depression, addiction and general mental health problems. By 2001 we were seeing up to 30 clients a week.

At that time the use of heroin was spreading rapidly in the area and causing havoc among vulnerable youngsters. The local medical profession was reluctant to introduce a needle exchange to avoid HIV and other infections, fearing that the service would encourage further drug use. In spite of the absence of specialist drug services in the town, many GPs were not using our counsellors so we decided to enhance our status by purchasing training to Diploma level. We were given a grant of £63,000 from the National Lottery Fund and trained eight counsellors to that level in 2001. GPs began to use the service.

There are, of course, many 'schools' of counselling, some more intrusive and directive than others. Having been involved with psychiatrists in my youth, I had an aversion to medical intervention and indeed to any controlling form of counselling. It was natural that we would be drawn towards the Person Centred approach developed by Carl Rogers, which is fundamentally democratic and unintrusive. The basic principle of this method is that the counsellor relates to the client with 'unconditional positive regard', listening without judging, and sharing the client's concerns without giving advice or direction. It is about being with the client and putting back to him his thoughts. In a sense, the client is listening to himself. On many occasions clients have said, 'Remember what you were saying last week . . .' when in fact they said it themselves. Sometimes there are long silences. I remember one client who came regularly and, for an hour, barely spoke. On one occasion I asked him as he was leaving if he found the sessions helpful. 'Oh yes,' he replied, 'it is great to talk to somebody.'

Just as there many schools of counselling so there are many species of counsellor. There is, for example, the lady counsellor with a long, diaphanous, tie-dyed skirt, a hand-knitted jumper, worry beads and sandals, who will be desperately kind and overflowing with sympathy. She will be there to make you feel better at all costs. There is the woman with a cadaverous face and intense, blazing eyes, whose life is so dull that she seeks excitement by listening to the suffering of others. There is the respectable man on a crusade to save the errant members of the community from eternal damnation. There are those searching for a purpose in their own lives and desperate to be liked. I have encountered many kinds, many of whom are genuine and some of whom are charlatans.

I have always been dedicated to the ethics involved in counselling, for it is by ethical practice that the safety and welfare of the client are protected. One of the great weaknesses of the system lies in supervision. For every few hours engaging with clients, counsellors should have an hour's supervision by a trained and experienced supervisor with whom they discuss their practice. The problem is that the supervisor relies entirely on the counsellor for the description and interpretation of the counselling sessions. The effectiveness of supervision depends on the integrity of the counsellor. I have never been comfortable with that.

In 2003, while she was engaged in research for a review of counselling in Scotland, we met Professor Liz Bondi from Edinburgh University who had come to interview us in Lorn Counselling Service. Having heard about our links with Iona, she commented that links with Iona were often mentioned in counselling circles, It is quite fascinating how the influence of that remote island community has spread to so many spheres of Scottish life.

The Counselling Service collapsed in 2008 due to serious mismanagement some years after Jan and I retired. Fortunately, by that time, some new services had started in the town so our clients were not completely deprived of vital help, but the offer of free, immediate counselling had vanished.

In my last year in Oban High School I took a group of youngsters to Northern Ireland as part of a course on 'Conflict Resolution'. We stayed in the Corrymeela Community not far from the Giant's Causeway. This is a remarkable centre founded in 1965 with the intention of providing a refuge for traumatised people forced out of their homes or surrounded by violence in Belfast or Derry. It was founded by Ray Davey and John Morrow, who was a member of the Iona Community. The centre is a beautiful building in a peaceful place, ideal for respite. The staff helped our students to understand how ordinary people suffered from the violence and why such a facility was vital to children witnessing bombings, rubber bullets, executions and knee-capping. We visited Hazelwood School in Belfast, an interde-nominational establishment, serving some of the most fractured townships in the city. Our youngsters were greatly impressed by the compassion and level of understanding of the staff and the easy relationships of the students. We visited a Trauma Centre in the Ardoyne, where the walls of one room were lined with photographs of local people who had been killed in the Troubles. It was an astonishing display, with portraits of children, young-sters, adults and elderly, bringing home to us the extent and range of the victims.

We were taken on a tour of the wall paintings in the city, a practice about which I have some doubts. There is something voyeuristic about it, as if the wounds of the communities are being paraded in front of us for our entertainment. The paint-ings are stark and provocative, designed to offend, to ignite the flames of hatred and bigotry. Not pieces of illustrious art to inspire reflection, wonderment or tranquillity. The paintings of Soviet Realism, like these, may be a form of propaganda but are not infused with such venom.

I think our young people learnt something from the visit. Certainly they seemed to have some understanding of the links between the Scottish football teams and the sectarian strife in

Northern Ireland and how opposing views can lead to extreme violence if conflict is not resolved. Perhaps, though, I overestimated the impact of the experience and they were merely reciting what they thought I would like to hear. Perhaps all they will remember is the Saint Patrick's Day parade and the ridiculous 'Paddy' hats with auburn wigs which they wore on the day.

When I return to the Province now I leave with a sense of despair. The fact that the inter-tribal violence has largely ceased is wonderful, but so many toxic remnants of the sectarian conflict can still be seen – the red, white and blue paving stones, the frames for the Orange arches, the tattered tricolours, the slogans, the provocative bonfires, the marches. These form a language of their own, a warning to the other tribe, a declaration of intent. It grieves me to think that my father's portrait appears on an Orange banner. I would be more hopeful if these public symbols of suspicion and antipathy withered away. Yet to deny the immense progress made in the Peace Process and the Good Friday Agreement and the magnificent efforts of the peacemakers would be surly and dishonest. Those achievements did create an atmosphere of hope and even optimism.

But new tremors are shaking the earth of Ulster which could threaten the entire edifice of accord constructed so carefully by the peacemakers. The decision of England and Wales to leave the European Union in 2016 has not only split Northern Ireland but has left the British government with an insoluble dilemma regarding the Border. Some Tory MPs are prepared to sacrifice the Good Friday agreement in order to gain a clean break with Europe. A clean break would mean the return of customs posts and every possibility of a revival of violence.

The tragedy is that the British government is now – in 2019 – in thrall to the Democratic Unionist Party, the most reactionary political party in the province, which always regarded Europe as a threat to its union with Britain and is pledged to leave the EU. It is obvious to anyone familiar with Ireland that the border must be kept open but it is clearly at risk of closure. It presents a difficult, if not intractable, problem, one which was barely mentioned in the referendum campaign. Logic dictates that, if Britain leaves the EU, there has to be a border somewhere – in Ireland or on mainland UK. The most obvious answer in Ireland is, of course, unification but that is a journey fraught with peril. David Cameron's 2016 referendum has left a trail of division, distrust, hostility and despair.

I am applying for an Irish passport so that I can travel freely in the country of my birth and within Europe. Like most Scots I voted to remain. Indeed every constituency in Scotland chose remain. I have no doubt that PB would have campaigned with the DUP to leave. The strange thing is that he was a devoted Francophile. Another of his contradictions.

18

PB received a few letters from colleagues in the House after his resignation, including one from his 'pair', Michael Foot,

> I will certainly miss you and I am sure Parliament will too . . . I know a little of what you contributed to the House of Commons, sometimes in very difficult circumstances. It was a real achievement.

Jim Molyneux wrote,

> At a recent meeting of the Coalition I was asked to thank you particularly for the great kindness you showed to successive generations of Ulster members arriving as new boys in this very confusing place. We all remember with deep gratitude the advice and guidance you gave to us all in our turn and certainly such success as some of us may have attained is due in no small measure to the grounding you gave us in the ways of the House and all its works.

Such appreciation colours one's view of his tragic private life.

As already mentioned, he took a job as a receptionist in a London hotel, which also provided accommodation, and then a position as a clerk with Titmus, Sainer and Webb, the solicitors.

By this time fortunately both of his parents, for whose approval he had always craved, had died, his father following his mother in 1967. His sister, Lassie, who had made every effort to persuade him to abandon his relationship with Julia and return to Marion, was horrified by the outcome.

Lassie had supported him throughout his career and was one of the few members of the family who knew of his illegitimate son, James. I imagine that she helped Marion through the difficult months of the pregnancy by providing advice and encouragement. Certainly none of Marion's family could help, as she insisted they were not to know. Lassie had been a close friend over the years. She and Marion had often shared holidays in Ireland with PB and his brother Robin, hiring a campervan which they called the 'Devilbile'. I did think it was a strange combination of characters, yet they seemed to enjoy the adventures.

Lassie, late in life aged 44, had married a minister, Richard Bannon, a kind, modest little man whose tonsured bald head and contented demeanour were reminiscent of those of a Columban monk. He was minister of Carnlough parish where Lassie's grandfather had been in charge and where her grandmother was buried. The couple moved into a new rectory with a magnificent view across the sea. Dickie, as we knew him, made the most potent primrose wine in the Province. I am not sure what he thought of PB's predicament or Lassie's peregrinations in the Devilbile but, knowing his patience and compassion, I imagine that he endured it all with monkish equanimity.

Two years after PB left Julia at the altar she had a serious car crash in which her five-year-old daughter was killed. Distraught, she turned to him for help and they were reunited. He moved into her flat overlooking the Thames and Blackfriar's Bridge. I visited them there on my way back from Russia and again when

Jan and I returned from Yugoslavia. Julia was always very keen to persuade us of his impecunity.

'Your father has no money,' was a sentence that rang out more than once. Clearly she thought that she was protecting him from his predatory children.

Some years later PB had a heart attack and had to have a triple bypass operation. Given his lifestyle while he was in Parliament, this is not surprising, as he had an appetite for good wine and expensive restaurants – a 'bon viveur' indeed. While he was in hospital Julia wrote one of the most moving love letters, which I have beside me, thanking him,

> for the millions of tendernesses, great and small which you have heaped everlastingly at my feet time and again . . . above all thank you for loving me and teaching me so painstakingly and patiently all those things that are in your heart and most precious to you . . . through tears I ask you to forgive each hurt that I may ever have done to you . . . come back to me quickly – restored or not.

He survived, recovered from surgery and lived with her for the rest of his life.

The politician who succeeded him in October 1974 was of course Enoch Powell who was elected with a reduced majority of 3,500, a reduction which surprised the Unionist management who had expected an overwhelming vote in Powell's favour. Powell had been manoeuvring for a seat in Ulster as a means of returning to Conservative politics in Westminster and the Unionists were very keen to add such a celebrity to their ranks.

The catastrophe of PB's 'marriage' in August 1974 provided the opportunity. Powell's biographer, Simon Heffer, in *Like the Roman*, suggests that, prior to this, influential Unionists were putting pressure on PB to stand down. If that was the case, PB was blissfully unaware of it till he resurfaced after 'doing the bunk'. When James Molyneux wrote to Powell on 21 August saying that there had been a 'dramatic development in the S. Down situation', PB had just informed him of his calamitous mistake and the inevitable consequences.

Up to that point PB had no intention of retiring. Certainly when he spent the previous Christmas with us he had every intention of carrying on with his political career. He was indeed in great spirits, entertaining our children with his prodigious appetite at a Chinese restaurant in Oban. He had a way with our children which did not surface with his own. They liked him enormously and found him wonderfully amusing. This was the other side of his character, one of which we glimpsed occasionally as children when he recited 'The Walrus and the Carpenter' or 'Jabberwocky' or read from the *Just So Stories*. He was very much at ease with our family that Christmas, the last before his sense of shame edged us apart.

Later that year PB's friend John Gorst, who had been involved with him in British Lion Films, launched the Middle Class Association, a right-wing organisation advocating lower taxes and individual liberty. PB had been working on this with Gorst and Julia but backed out of any direct commitment after August, although he wrote a letter to *The Times* in January 1975 defending the organisation. In any case the organisation quickly faded and died.

He retired to the country where he fed the birds, looked after the garden and kept house for Julia who drove down from London at weekends.

He died on the 12th of July (of course!) 1991. The funeral was a bizarre occasion. It was held in an ancient twelfth-century church in Wiltshire, where the Special Branch officers, skulking behind yew trees and as inconspicuous as lady boys, outnumbered the mourners. They were assigned to the ceremony, I think, to guard Jim Molyneux, the only one of PB's former colleagues to attend. Even Michael Foot, for years his 'pair' in the House of Commons, had a prior engagement.

I did see him before he died, travelling down to Swindon where he was by train. A small, fragile figure slumped in a chair with his chin on his chest, he slept much of the time during my visit – I have that effect on people. He woke a couple of times clearly terrified of the demons in his dreams. He did wake enough at one point to recognise me and to chat casually about trivialities – with one exception.

'We never did talk together, did we?' he said.

A deep regret on both parts.

As I left the ward I looked back and he raised a hand in farewell. I never saw him again.

Still, I have his son, my secret half-brother, to remind me of him. The resemblance is striking. Bearing the name of PB's brother who was drowned, James was born in 1955 and lives in France. He was adopted shortly after birth and brought up on a farm in England. His existence was successfully concealed from all of us till 2013 when he made the effort to contact me – the magic of the internet!

19

Having been convinced at the age of eighteen that I would not live to see twenty, I was astonished to discover that I was sixty at the millennium. Jan arranged a surprise for my birthday which fortunately fell in the school holidays. Unknown to me, she booked flights to Dublin, accommodation in a hotel and hire of a car. Returning to the scenes of my youth in my favourite city was a wonderful gift. Dublin, though, had changed. It is still a beautiful place with the elegant Georgian houses, the dark river Liffey, the green garden squares and the wide sweep of O'Connell Street, but it had become so seriously congested that traffic came to a standstill during our visit. Still, we managed to see a performance of *Arms and the Man* in the Gate Theatre, the venue where both myself and my mother had appeared. Sadly, when I enquired after the actors whom I had admired, they were dead – Dermot Tuohy, Maureen Delaney, Shelagh Richards and Aidan Grenell. The girl at the desk, sensing my disappointment, assured me kindly that Aidan's son worked regularly at the Gate – a reminder of my age and mortality.

We left Dublin and drove west into Tipperary, searching for the hamlet of Ballybrit, the birthplace of my grandfather's mother, Mary Drought. Having little success, I enquired at a local petrol station but the attendant had no knowledge of the family. However a gnarled old farmer drove in on his tractor for fuel and, as he had a hay tedder behind the tractor, we fell into conversation about the harvest. When I asked him if he had heard of Mary Drought, he took me by the arm and pointed to a field on the hill.

'You see that wee field? Your great grandmother rented it to my great grandmother.'

A small island is Ireland.

We drove into Connemara – just as my parents had done before the war in their horse-drawn caravan. It has a wild, captivating beauty reminiscent of western Sutherland. I can understand why artists such as Paul Henry were drawn to its grandeur. Though the white thatched cottages and turf stacks of his time have largely been replaced by modern bungalows, the country is still magnificent. When we reached Westport we could see a long stream of people ascending and descending one of the mountains – not a sight seen in Scotland. The mountain, of course, was Croagh Patrick and the people were Catholic pilgrims. Westport itself was crowded with them, some recovering from the climb in their bare feet. Such mass devotion and self-harm is both astonishing and confusing. In one sense, such a feat of endurance is admirable; in another, it is beyond comprehension that human beings imagine that self-inflicted pain can wash away mental and physical misdemeanours. Still, it is an ancient concept and one which seems to last in religious circles.

As we toured the south we noticed the proliferation of large new houses, often thrusting ostentatious gateways towards the road. Enquiring whether these were built by wealthy Europeans or Americans, we were told that they belonged to native Irish people who had returned home. When we asked how their confidence in Ireland had been restored, the unanimous answer was not, as we expected, joining the EEC but 'getting out from under'. Independence. A lesson there for Scots?

We travelled north to Sligo and parked on the shores of Lough Gill where I remembered my father's love of Yeats and the romantic side of his nature. With the sun glittering on the quiet lake water and the larks rising in song above the hills, it was not difficult to relive the evenings spent there when I was a boy. We visited Gartan where Columba of Iona was born and about which the beautiful song 'The Gartan Mother's Lullaby' was written and arranged by Herbert Hughes. Naturally, we had to see the grave of Yeats in Drumcliff churchyard. That was a disappointing experience as the site had become a tourist attraction with buses and information boards, somehow conflicting with the poet's epitaph written by him in 1938 and inscribed on the headstone:

> Cast a cold eye
> On life, on death.
> Horseman, pass by!

The final visit was to the graveyard in Carnlough where my relatives are buried. It is sad that PB lies in a grave on the other side of the Irish Sea in the little English village of Lydiard Millicent. I doubt if any one visits it. He should have been buried with his people. His grandmother, Kate Story, lies here with his mother, father, brother and sister.

One of the great disappointments of my life was the election of Tony Blair. I remember the euphoria when the result was announced, with people out in the village street celebrating. The Iraq War and his intimacy with business tycoons shattered our illusions. We joined a march in Oban against the war, attended by an extraordinary array of people from elderly gentlefolk to young mothers with prams. Most of them had never been on a march. My daughter Erin and her husband took their children on the Glasgow march and we all watched the million protesters in London. Blair did not listen. Then we saw the 'Shock and Awe' in Iraq and recoiled in horror and disbelief. During the war I wrote these lines,

> There is a rat gnawing the floor in the corner.
> Hearing it, I know I am not dead.
> If I lie still, the pain may pass.
> The long bones of my legs gleam in the moonlight
> And the hole in my side is numb and black
> And the blood on the floor is cold.
> Out on the street many are dead –
> The ploughman's eyes will stare at the sky
> Till the birds are sure of his death;
> The tailor's deft fingers
> Will clutch forever the unbending earth
> A sabre's length from his arm.
> Who will turn the furrow now
> Or keep the seams straight?
> Christ save us they must run out of fools sometime.
> Out on the hill the Lords of the Manor
> Try to rally their ghosts –
> They were so sure that they were right.
> Brown rat, gnawing the floor,
> When you gnaw at me eat first my heart –

Its anger is more painful than my wounds.

The appalling consequences of that war are with us still in Syria, Libya, Yemen. I am glad that we marched and did what we could to oppose it.

Nearing retirement, I returned to the passion of my ill-spent youth, renewing my interest in theatre – always a risky business as, like knotgrass, it is desperately invasive and tends to take over the unwary participant's entire waking hours. First, I wrote and directed a play for Argyll Youth Theatre based on the Famine in the Ross of Mull, with my grandson playing the unenviable part of Trevelyan. We took it on tour, visiting Tobermory, Bunessan, Appin and Oban, an experience reminiscent of the pandemonium of the Irish tours. The main problem was not, as one might expect, that of keeping the boys from the girls' bedrooms but rather the other way round. It was an exhausting but thoroughly enjoyable tour and some of the youngsters have gone on to drama college and careers in theatre.

I also wrote and directed a one-act play for a local theatre group which was set in India at the time of partition and based on a short story by Jhumpa Lahiri called 'A Real Durwan'. Sadly, some of our Bengalis could not lose their Highland accent so it did not win at the Drama Festival. I continued to help with other productions until the typical internal disputes of AmDram became too tedious to endure.

I did finish another play about the six Mitford sisters, the staging of which came to a sad end. It is not widely known that Unity Mitford died in Oban in 1948. Renowned for her infatuation with Hitler and his Nazi Party, she attempted suicide in

Germany when war was declared in 1939. The bullet lodged in her brain and Hitler was so concerned that he arranged her transport back to England. The injury left her seriously disabled. Her mother, Lady Redesdale, wanted to take her to their island of Inchkenneth off Mull for recuperation, but the Government prevented this on the grounds of national security. However, after the war, she was granted permission and Unity returned to the island, remaining there for most of her remaining days. Her sister, Diana, who married Oswald Mosley and was imprisoned with her husband during the war, often visited her on the island. Decca emigrated to America and joined the Communist Party there, robustly opposing Diana's release from prison. Nancy became an author and lived in France. Deborah married the Duke of Devonshire and Pamela, unlike her sisters, lived a quiet life in the countryside with her companion Giuditta Tommasi. A fascinating family and, because of the connections with Oban and Mull, I wrote a play about the girls. Rehearsals were going well until the director left the group and then one of the leading ladies departed. The play languishes in a drawer beside me.

I continue to write. It is an infection which lingers on the skin like staphylococcus. Being a solitary occupation, it is not popular with those who share the household. I persist nevertheless. On one occasion I almost abandoned the habit. When I first read Virginia Woolf the brilliance of her writing was so intimidating and eclipsed my efforts so completely that I lapsed into silence for years. Now, when I read Eimear McBride and see her rise to fame, I wonder if I should continue. Mind you, her writing is reminiscent of J.P. Dunleavy's, so perhaps tastes move in circles and there will be a revival of more conventional styles.

We have seen many changes over the years, particularly in Scottish farming. Gone are the binders, the travelling mills, corn stacks, hay rucks and horse rakes – all consigned to folk museums and history books. Shepherds no longer walk round the flocks in horsehide sprung boots but whizz about on quad bikes with their dogs riding pillion. Gone are the organo-phosphate dips, carbon tetrachloride fluke drenches, hand shears, wool bags, branding irons and burdizzos for castration. The system of neighbouring, where herds from adjoining hirsels would get together to gather and work with their flocks, has largely disappeared as hills were sold off for forestry and work was contracted out. That loss has weakened many remote communities.

However, the greatest change has been in land reform. Having been in farming since 1961 and having been a farming tenant as well as an historian, my interest in the land law was inevitable. When I first read *The Highland Clearances* by John Prebble I was infuriated by the injustices inflicted by a rich and powerful landowner on defenceless people. This anger inspired a craving for greater knowledge of the outrage. Prebble's influence on the revival of Scottish history has often been underestimated, particularly by later academics, but there is no doubt that the clarity of his writing and his polemic made history accessible. People realised that they had been deprived of the greatest part of their past. True, Tom Johnston's *History of the Working Classes in Scotland* in 1946 paved the way, but Prebble's popular books unleashed an unstoppable flood of research which has transformed Scottish politics and land law. Jim Hunter's *The Making of the Crofting Community* portrayed the suffering and the long struggle for justice of the Gaels in the Highlands.

The first attack on the landowning elite was launched by the crofting communities in the Crofting Wars of the 1880s. Organised in the Highland Land Law Reform Association they won the Crofters Holdings (Scotland) Act of 1886, guaranteeing security of tenure, fair rent and compensation for improvements. The Act did not threaten the ownership of land. There were subsequent pieces of legislation which enhanced tenants' rights but the establishment of a Scottish Parliament has been the major factor in transforming land law in Scotland. The Labour government had led the way with the Crofting Reform (Scotland) Act of 1976, giving crofters the right to buy their land, but the first act of the new Scottish parliament was to abolish feudal tenures and impositions. That was a shot across the bows of the landowners' galleon. Then came the Land Reform (Scotland) Act of 2003 with the public access to land enshrined, the right of communities to buy land and enhanced crofting rights. Further strength was added in 2015 with the Community Empowerment Act which included urban land in the right to buy and, more recently, the Land Reform Act of 2016 which gave further protection to tenant farmers and gave ministers the power to compel the sale of land to communities in the interests of 'sustainable development'. This raft of radical legislation, which has shifted the balance of power in favour of communities, was only made possible by devolution and the levers of power being transferred to the Scottish people.

Since 1993 several large estates have been handed to community trusts, the first of these being the 22,000 acres of Assynt. Following that the islanders of Eigg raised £1.5 million to buy their land in 1997. Other communities have used the new laws to take control of their destinies: Abriachan, Knoydart, Isle Martin, Gigha, North Harris, Langamull and Cultybraggan in Comrie. The latest bid is from the islanders of Ulva, which had been virtually cleared of its people during the famine of the 1840s. Perhaps the stone walls of the deserted townships, which still stand as a memorial to the evicted families, will be rebuilt and the island return to prosperity.

The 'buy-out' which received the most publicity involved two friends of ours – Tom Forsyth and Bob Harris. Along with Alastair McIntosh, who now works for GalGael, and Liz Lyon, they formed the Eigg Heritage Trust in 1991 to raise funds for the islanders. One of the first contributors was John Harvey, the leader of the Iona Community. I was asked to contribute but I confess that what we had to spare went to *Medecins sans Frontières*. At the time Eigg was owned by a flamboyant southern industrialist called Keith Schellenberg. Formerly an Olympic bobsleigh champion and powerboat enthusiast, he was portrayed as a 'Toad of Toad Hall' character, racing round the island in his 1927 Rolls-Royce wearing goggles and a tweed jacket. Having bought his dream island in 1975, he did set out to improve it with the help of a grant from the HIDB. Initially fired with enthusiasm, he renovated buildings, enticed settlers from the mainland, opened a tearoom and craft centre and bought a motor yacht to seduce visitors. The population increased from 39 to 60 by 1979 with 12 children in the school. Sadly, the idyll turned sour.

His former wife laid claim to her share of the island and his relationship with the islanders began to pall as the behaviour of the 'hooray-henrys' invited to his estate as guests became more outrageous and offensive. Schellenberg turned out to be as capricious and as insensitive as his friends. He paid off some of the settlers he had enticed to the island and abandoned the renovations. In 1992 he sold the island to another dubious character who claimed to be a distinguished artist and professor. Just what the island needed. Gotthilf Christian Eckhard Oesterle who liked to be known as Maruma was actually unknown in the art world and his claim to wealth was as fictitious as his doctorate. Eventually he too was forced to sell Eigg – this time to the islanders. I was asked again to contribute to the Trust but politely declined.

Schellenberg's wife, Suki Urquhart, had a genuine affection for the island, restoring the lodge and the gardens. She was said to have a brilliant eye for colour, shape and setting, regarding the creation of a garden as a painting. After she left the island she moved to Edinburgh where she started to write about gardening and eventually published the popular *Scottish Gardener* with Birlinn in 2005. She divorced Schellenberg in 1997.

There is still much to be done in the field of land reform. Proprietors can still find ways of prohibiting public access and evicting tenants. In the late nineteenth and early twentieth centuries there was an argument in socialist circles between those who advocated 'peasant proprietorship' and those who supported 'state ownership'. While I worked for the Department of Agriculture and saw many of its holdings granted to deserving tenants, I was of the opinion that state ownership was the only way to counter the power of landlords. The Department helped many young shepherds to have their own farms while insisting that they had the experience and knowledge to make them successful. Now, however, I see the value of community owner-ship – I hesitate to use the term 'peasant proprietors'.

As a member of an ethnic minority and refugee from the tribal warfare in Ulster, I have always regarded the Scots as a tolerant, egalitarian and compassionate people. I suspect that many of their characteristics stem from the collectives of the heavy industries and crofting communities and the long struggle for justice and equality. The response to appeals for aid has always been noticeably more generous than that of neighbour-ing countries. Because of that I feel at home in Scotland. That is not to say there are not putrefying pockets of bigotry, abuse and exploitation, but fortunately they are rare and largely invisible.

When I first sailed up to the Broomielaw in 1959 I was struck by the number of ships moored on the quays and the vast array of shipyards on the Clyde. The hulls of half-built ships cradled in scaffolding, the skeletons of ore cranes, the blue flashes of welding torches, the deafening rattle of riveting. Glasgow was an industrial city then. The elegant buildings were black with soot and the air smelt of sulphur. I took the train to Oban travelling through Larbert, Callander, Balquhidder and Crianlarich, stunned by the magnificent scenery. I had never seen majestic mountains like Ben More and Stob Binnein, Beinn Laoigh and Cruachan. I had climbed Slieve Donard and Errigal with my father and peered with him over the cliffs of Slieve League, but the first sight of that Highland landscape is imprinted on my memory.

Iona was a remote island at that time with no car ferry. MacBrayne's boat from Oban anchored off Craignure and passengers had to leap into a smaller red boat to be ferried ashore at the old jetty. From there Bowman's buses carried them across Mull to Fionnphort where a small open boat, manned by two stalwart seamen, waited to take them to Iona. The single-track road across Mull at that time was narrow and hazardous with grass growing in the middle. I remember on one occasion the bus driver had spent a little too much time in a hostelry and, as we headed west, the bus, with increasing frequency, veered off the road into the heather. Eventually, halfway across the island, the driver stopped, burst into tears and admitted that he could go no further. We were aghast. There we were, isolated in the middle of the glen, having no idea how to get home. By an extraordinary coincidence one of the passengers possessed a PSV licence and we were able to proceed with the driver weeping behind him and repeating endlessly his profuse apologies. That was in 1960, the dream time.

Now Iona is no longer remote. Fleets of buses brimming with tourists descend on the island daily, crossing on the car ferry from Oban to Mull and from Mull to Iona. It is possible for an islander to board their car on the island and drive to London. Broadband connects Iona to the world. In our time we had to go through the local telephone exchange and it was said that the operator there knew that a woman was pregnant before her husband.

Mull has changed too. Although there had been several salmon stations fishing with bag nets at Camas, Lochbuie and Calgary, there is now an array of thriving salmon farms and hatcheries creating vital employment. This industry has transformed the Highlands, allowing many young people to remain in remote communities who otherwise would have been forced to leave. Farmed salmon is now Scotland's largest food export, selling in more than 50 countries and employing more than 1,380 people full-time. On the Ross of Mull there is a fleet of small boats fishing for shellfish, most of which is sent to Europe. It is astonishing to see lorries loading at Bunessan pier, knowing that the next stop will be Spain. Scottish shellfish production is now worth nearly £12 million. Some of the larger projects have been started by incomers. Jeff Reade from Somerset took over a derelict farm near Tobermory in 1983 and transformed it into a very successful dairy farm producing Isle of Mull cheese. I had passed the farm every day in 1967 when I was self-employed and dreamt about restoring it. Another incomer, James Knight, started a quarry which has diversified into construction and is one of the most prominent businesses in the area.

The changes which we have seen in Mull are reflected elsewhere in the Highlands. We have seen remote communities benefit from electrification, new roads, small industries, much of this supported by the EU and the Scottish Government. The catalysts have undoubtedly been these two elements – devolution and EU membership. It is true that the oil industry has had a major impact on the area, extending to the Hebrides, but much of it is confined to the east coast. Devolution has provided a stimulus missing since the war, seen in the Road Equivalent Tariff for ferries and sustainable energy development such as wind and wave power generation.

Devolution is seen by many as a step towards independence, a goal which we have supported since we lived in Mull. In 1967 Iain MacCormick, later to become SNP MP for Argyll, came to see us on our farm at Saorphin. He had strong connections with the area. His predecessors came from Iona and his great uncle John had not only published the first Gaelic novel, *Dun-Aluinn*, but had started the Iona Press. His father, John MacDonald MacCormick, was a founder member of the SNP and its first national secretary. Since leaving Ireland I had avoided politics, having seen how poisonous involvement could be, but Iain's gentle manner and good sense persuaded us to join his party and so I became a Nationalist, a term which was anathema to PB and his family – they could never distinguish between the SNP and the IRA.

Now I live in a nation struggling to choose its place on the roulette wheel of a spinning world, whether to place its bet on independence or union, Europe or globalisation. Some would see the choice as freedom or bondage. England has chosen to leave Europe, a decision driven by emotion rather than reason, ignorance rather than enlightenment. PB opposed membership of the EEC because he feared it might lead to Irish unity and would probably have voted with the DUP in its campaign to leave. Yet I know he regarded with distaste Ian Paisley's provocative rhetoric and flirtation with violence, and his legacy, the DUP, which presently holds the British government to ransom, could determine the fate of Scotland. I imagine that many Scots, our family included, will view that with resentment if not anger and, if the people are hauled in a direction which they did not choose, our hope is that the case for independence will become irresistible.

I am convinced that the Scots are capable of building a nation in which the values of tolerance, compassion, fairness, equality and democracy are cherished. I have seen Ireland grow from an impoverished, introverted, religiously oppressed country into a nation which is prosperous and respected. I saw the poverty in the streets of Dublin and Cork in 1958 and know how far the Republic has travelled since then. I have seen the election of the first female president and now a gay Taoiseach, Leo Varadkar, the son of Hindu doctor. If the same energy for change was let loose in Scotland, it could be 'a nation again'.

Now that I am nearing four-score years I look back over the years since the War and wonder what has made me who I am. In my youth I launched into every risk available at that time and might well have had a shorter life had I not been rescued by the love of a very patient woman. I try to excuse the years of self-indulgence by claiming that I felt I deserved a reward for the unravelling of my parents' marriage, and yet it is a lame explanation and probably false. True, we were feral children without many boundaries and I enjoyed every minute of the freedom, but it was in that freedom that I got lost, that the glue which held me together as a person melted and I disintegrated. That was a dark, terrifying and painful time, but it may have been the experience which gave me the insight and empathy to help damaged, disturbed and disaffected people.

Believing in nurture not nature, I imagine that many people have influenced my growth, some helpfully and some destructively. My grandmother, PB's mother, not only gave unconditional love but showed me that caring for others was a virtue. Having spent so much time with her and my grandfather in Gilford, I must have absorbed some of their Christian views. Certainly I have vivid memories of his church and morning prayers on our knees in his study. PB provided the values which

I learnt to shun, the icon to be cast down. He found it difficult to show affection and was absent for much of my life. Yet I appreciated his charm and wit. My mother, for all her faults, encouraged our creative interests in music, theatre and literature and these have been passed on to two of our grandchildren – one a musician, the other an actor. My errant uncle Robin, the 'black sheep', provided the rebellious figure necessary to any boy's childhood, the hero prepared to challenge the norms, the man with the machismo. In the confusion of adolescence many models flickered in front of me, from James Dean to Randy Turpin, from Bill Haley to Gigli, from Spam to Anew McMaster. In the midst of this appeared Carlo Piezner, the leader of a Rudolf Steiner community in Ireland, whose shadow remained with me for many years. After the breakdown, George MacLeod and people connected with the Iona Community were sources of inspiration – Tom Forsyth who introduced me to Gurdjieff, Tony Dickens who pointed me towards Zen Buddhism, Ronnie Laing who convinced me that my 'breakdown' was a natural stage of development and Tom Buchan who showed me that humour was an acceptable, if not vital, part of literature.

Given my strong connections with Iona and the proliferation of ministers in the family, it might be assumed that I am a Christian, but many members of the established churches would be horrified by any suggestion of my association with their faith. Although many of my early years were spent with my grandparents in Gilford and I attended church there, my commitment to their religion was largely superficial, a gesture of respect rather than a conviction. When I suffered the darkness and confusion of mental illness, I found neither solace nor solution in their Christian philosophy. Like many of our contemporaries, I searched through Buddhism, Zen, the *Tao Te Ching*, the *Bhagavad Gita*, Theosophy, the *Quran*, Gnosticism and the Dead Sea Scrolls and found no complete answer. I am a devout agnostic, accepting that I cannot know. The derivation, nature and meaning of the force which drives the cycle of life and death on earth remain a mystery. What lies beyond is pure conjecture or a matter of belief. The ancient Greeks had an altar to the unknown god and I suppose I might have worshipped there. Yet, when the blizzards on the hill whipped my oilskin leggings and tore at my coat, I sometimes shook my fist at the sky and cursed it.

I am the result of so many influences – people, locations, events, accidents, coincidences. Battered by fate, moulded by ideas, stitched by people, energised by emotions, I sometimes wonder how much of the creature is my creation. I do not believe in predestination or the will of Allah. I have made choices – some quite disastrous – but, in comparison with the choices made for me, most of them seem less significant. When I try to analyse my father – what made him who he became – he is still a mystery. As a child he was shaped by the faith of his parents. His siblings were sure that he thought of himself as superior. At school he was regarded as bookish – what today would be called a 'geek' – but his enrolment in the Eton of Ulster separated him from his siblings and his home. Campbell College, as intended, reinforced his sense of superiority as did his sojourn with the Life Guards – allowing him to keep the title of 'Captain'. He admired Churchill and Powell and tried to emulate their rhetoric in the House, but their influence was always diluted by his life outside Parliament – his foray to Russia or his entanglements in England. Perhaps what shaped him most was his appearance. Being so handsome allowed him to charm both men and women but also, as Fate would have it, led to his political demise. He should have learnt from the legend of Narcissus.

On the few occasions when our children met him, they found him 'great fun', but they are very conscious of his flaws. One of our tasks has been to protect our children from our parents.

Answering a request to speak to the people about children, Kahlil Gibran's prophet says,

> Your children are not your children.
> They are the sons and daughters of Life's longing for itself.
> They come through you but not from you,
> And, though they are with you yet they belong not to you . . .
> You may house their bodies but not their souls . . .
> You may strive to be like them, but seek not to make them like you . . .
> You are the bows from which your children as living arrows are sent forth.

We had read Gibran before we were married and adopted his approach to children. We have watched them grow with astonishment and admiration. Astonishment because we had neither a textbook on child-rearing nor a shining example in our parents and therefore had to follow our instincts – our eldest son has always maintained that he was an experiment. Admiration because we appreciated their resilience in coping with our nomadic existence and our mistakes. We encouraged them to be themselves with their own views and values and not to follow the herd. At times they suffered from this at school as some teachers resented their independence. We tried to avoid imposing on them our values and way of life and that was one of the reasons for leaving the islands. We wanted them to have the opportunity to choose a different path – to become businessmen, venture capitalists, soldiers, even Tories if they wished.

One has become a structural engineer, married to a girl from Iona whose mother we knew when we first arrived on the island. Another a forensic social worker in a secure unit, another a lecturer in criminology and sociology and another, who trained in Art College as a jewellery designer and ran a chain of shops, is now a lawyer. All very different, as we hoped.

Sadly, we have lost the son who was born on Mull. Jamie had emigrated to Australia, his second marriage being to an Australian girl whose parents were Turkish, He alternated between two professions in Sydney – sometimes a motorbike mechanic and sometimes an operating theatre technician in hospital, qualified as both. He contracted a brain tumour and, in spite of surgery and various therapies, died in March 2016, leaving three teenage boys. We were proud of the way he dealt with the illness, showing extraordinary courage and dignity. He is buried in a Muslim cemetery in Sydney, a plot which, in spite of the Islamic inscription on the tombstone, will always remain part of Scotland. When he was ill our daughter arranged with the Scottish Rugby XV to send him a jersey signed by the team. That was his most precious possession. The loss of a son, as my grandmother knew, is a cruel blow from which it is difficult to recover. My great regret is that I was unable to see him before he died. Part of our lives ended then. Memory is a poor substitute for the real person.

Yet, in these pages, I have moved through a forest of memories – some vivid, some dim, some bright, some dark, some simmering with laughter, some silent with sorrow. If I had to choose one of my father, it would not be one of his portrait on an Orange banner, but of his dark eyes fixed on the rise of a trout in an Antrim stream and the whistle of his split-cane rod in the dusk, an image of the man he might have been. Memories will shimmer and fade, curl like old photos, mutate into myths, develop into demons, deceive and mock us as we fight to cling to them. Yet, in the end, they are all that we have. I treasure three.

One of a girl sitting on the white sand of Iona, her long fair hair glinting in the sun. Behind her, the wind whistles in the marram grass and carves crescents in the sand with the sharp points. White gulls wheel over the sapphire sea and sandpipers scuttle along the tide-edge. The colour of her eyes matches the sea. The memory brings a feeling of warmth and gladness.

Another of a summer's dawn on the summit of Beinn Dhucraig with a mantle of webs over the heather glistening in the rising sun. A herd of hinds disappears over the ridge, hooves rattling in the scree. A grouse clucks in the glen below and a dog-fox barks for his vixen in the corrie. Remembering the scene brings nostalgia and sadness, for I will never see the summits again.

The third of Piskariovskoe cemetery in Leningrad where the flame of remembrance burns in memory of the 630,000 who died during the Siege defending their city against the Nazi invasion. Many died of starvation and hypothermia. In front of the flame, the cemetery stretches into the distance, line after line of gravestones and trees planted to remember the dead, citizens and soldiers. My father's brother risked his life on a warship escorting convoys bound for Murmansk and I like to think that, in a small way, he helped to save the city. The memory brings a feeling of defiance, a determination to see right triumph over wrong. When Shostakovich, during the siege, assembled his band of starving and freezing musicians and played his 7th Symphony over loudspeakers towards the Nazi lines, that was true defiance. That was magnificent.

I am still a socialist, a democrat, a nationalist, a republican, a dreamer, a grumpy old man and still, for old time's sake, I buy the *Morning Star*. My horsehide tackety boots hang in the shed to remind me of the herding days and I keep the crook that I carved from the horn of a Blackface tup.

Acknowledgements

I have many people to thank for their help with this publication. I would like to thank Stephen Mansfield for use of his excellent photographs; Francois Vincent of the *Banbridge Chronicle* for tracing speeches of Enoch Powell; Gilbert Paton for the photo of the Garth House Cricket team; Angela Hughes for allowing me to quote from *Chelsea Footprints*; Simon Heffer for references in *Like The Roman – the Life of Enoch Powell*; I must also mention Anne Cadwallader's *Lethal Allies*; and my boyhood friend, the late Paddy Ashdown, who remembered idyllic days in his autobiography. I wish also to thank John Tuckwell of John Donald for publishing my first two non-fiction books, *Deer Forests, Landlords* and *Crofters and Discovering Argyll, Mull and Iona*. I am grateful to Tom Johnstone in Birlinn for his patience and belief in this project – without him the MS would never have proceeded. Most of all, however, I must thank the person who tolerated my restlessness and misdemeanours and became my most valued critic – my wife and best friend.